⁀rom the reviews of *Comrade Jim*:

'Jim Riordan drops us into the bizarre, almost Gulliver-like ⁀vorld of the Cold War Soviet Union and its improbable cast of ⁀ootballers, spies and hard-line but dreamy-eyed communists. ⁀ makes both them and it vividly real and fascinating. So ⁀raordinary that you'll blink with disbelief when you read it'
DUNCAN HAMILTON, author of *Provided You Don't Kiss Me*

'This charming book encompasses all those elements that help ⁀nake a modern bestseller – espionage, treachery, class warfare, ⁀litics, celebrity, drink, nostalgia and . . . football'
Literary Review

⁀his strong and individual story makes for a good read'
Waterstone's Books Quarterly

⁀An] absorbing account of the big time seen from within through ⁀ie eyes of an enthusiastic amateur, laced with self-deprecation ⁀nd vast quantities of vodka'
Irish Times

⁀Had this wonderful book been a work of fiction it may have been deemed too incredible for publication . . . A genre-defying rollercoaster literary ride . . . Without a red card in sight, the only quibble this reviewer has with this entertaining book is its brevity. Please Jim, could we have some more?'
Sunday Tribune

By the same author

NOVELS FOR YOUNG PEOPLE
Sweet Clarinet
When the Guns Fall Silent
The Prisoner
War Song
Match of Death
The Cello
The Gift
Rebel Cargo

OTHER CHILDREN'S BOOKS
The Young Oxford Book of Football Stories
The Young Oxford Book of Sports Stories
The Young Oxford Book of War Stories
Russian Folk Tales
The Sun Maiden and the Crescent Moon
Siberian Folk Tales

JIM RIORDAN

Comrade Jim

THE SPY WHO PLAYED FOR SPARTAK

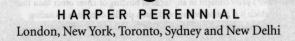

HARPER PERENNIAL
London, New York, Toronto, Sydney and New Delhi

Harper Perennial
An imprint of HarperCollins*Publishers*
77–85 Fulham Palace Road
Hammersmith
London W6 8JB
www.harperperennial.co.uk

Visit our authors' blog at www.fifthestate.co.uk
Love this Book? www.bookarmy.com

This Harper Perennial edition published 2009

1

First published in Great Britain by Fourth Estate in 2008

A catalogue record for this book is available from the British Library

ISBN 978-0-00-725115-5

Set in Minion with Helvetica display by
Newgen Imaging Systems (P) Ltd, Chennai, India

Printed and bound in Great Britain by Clays Ltd, St Ives plc

Mixed Sources
Product group from well-managed
forests and other controlled sources
www.fsc.org Cert no. SW-COC-1806
© 1996 Forest Stewardship Council

FSC

For my children:
Tania, Nadine, Sean, Nathalie and Catherine

CONTENTS

Introduction   1

1. War Boy   7
2. The Beautiful Russian Game   19
3. The Dartmoor Russki   33
4. Onwards and Upwards   41
5. Going Home   59
6. Moscow Realities   77
7. A Body to be Protected   85
8. The British in Moscow   97
9. Playing for the Home Side   107
10. Long Shadows on Moscow Grounds   155
11. The Amazing Life of Nikolai Starostin   177
12. Going Home   197

Acknowledgements   213
Index   215

INTRODUCTION

It never occurred to me that my 'loan spell' with Moscow Spartak warranted more than a line home. 'That's nice for you, Bill,' Mum'd say, no doubt taking Spartak to be a branch of Spar grocery stores. She'd warned me about going to Russia: 'You'll end up down those salt mines!' The thought of her son playing in the Lenin Stadium before some 50,000 people was as fanciful as him having tea with the Queen.

Then there was the 'class warrior' business. Playing for a commie team was something to keep under my hat. As an envoy of the British Communist Party at the Moscow Higher Party School – and you couldn't get higher than that in the communist education hierarchy – I had to draw a veil over my doings in the Soviet capital. But an even stronger fetter bound my tongue. Only six years earlier I'd learned Russian during National Service to spy on the Russians in Berlin, and I'd signed the Official Secrets Act to keep quiet about it. Now I was a two-timer, a double agent, albeit much inferior to real spies, like my Moscow comrades Guy Burgess and Donald Maclean.

Although I didn't know it at the time, under Stalin the Soviet secret police had shot people for less. Yes, I accept: *I should have known*. There are many things, looking back, that I curse myself for not knowing. Ignorance is no excuse. Uncle

Joe had died in 1953, a mere seven years before my arrival in Moscow. With his ghost still haunting every home, and his body beside Lenin's in the Red Square Mausoleum, it was not for me to cast a shadow over Moscow Spartak FC for risking their No. 5 shirt on an English back. In those days, you never knew whether the Stalinists would make a comeback, despite Khrushchov's condemnation of his predecessor's crimes.

You could see why the Spartak coach, Nikita Simonyan, had no wish to trumpet my debut as the first (and last) English-man to play for a premier Moscow team in the Lenin Stadium. As far as I knew, no player in Soviet league football had been born outside the USSR. I was the sole exception. What is more, though a comrade, I was not regarded as being entirely trustworthy, being from a *kapstran*, a 'capitalist country'. I was never permitted, for instance, to attend Party meetings at the Higher Party School or, later, at Progress Publishers where I worked for three years.

Incredibly (though was, or is, anything 'incredible' in Russia?), twenty years earlier, the erstwhile Soviet and Spartak football captain (and now general manager), Nikolai Starostin, along with his three brothers, had been sentenced to ten years' hard labour in a Siberian gulag for their foreign links or, as the official charge read, for trying 'to instil into our sport the mores of the capitalist world'. It did not matter that he was captaining a Soviet team sent to play against the French communist l'Etoile Rouge. These minor details tended to be overlooked.

World War II had enhanced suspicion of foreigners to the point of xenophobia, which resulted in government-sponsored campaigns to tarnish Soviet-based foreigners as the unwelcome bearers of 'rootless cosmopolitanism'. The net drew in most of the British communists I worked with later as a translator, and especially many Jews. Collaboration, even friendship, with foreigners was not to be encouraged. The Spartak staff were taking a huge risk in allowing the guest appearance of someone who wasn't *nash* – 'ours'. No wonder they kept it all hush-hush.

Why did they risk it? The early 1960s were risk-taking times: for poetry and prose, films and pop music, diplomatic forays abroad, including Party boss Khrushchov's trip to Hollywood, the first invitations to American jazz bands, like the Benny Goodman Orchestra, and wider sports contests, like the biennial athletics competition with the USA first held in Moscow in 1972. At times of change, bold Russians invariably tried to push boundaries further.

One more reason for caution was the international situation. In the early 1960s, the Cold War was at its coldest. In mid-1960, a summit meeting between Soviet leader Nikita Khrushchov and US President Eisenhower was aborted after the shooting down of an American U-2 spy plane well inside Soviet air space, and the subsequent trial of its pilot Gary Powers. Then came the Cuban Missile Crisis in October 1962 which brought the world closer to the brink of nuclear disaster than most people realized at the time. For several weeks, we Muscovites, no less than Westerners, anxiously tuned in to radio bulletins every half-hour, expecting the worst. If anything were to boil over, we would be first in the firing line. I could hardly hold up a white flag once the balloon went up and shout, 'Spare me, I'm British!'

All this further reinforced a morbid fear of foreigners, *any* foreigners.

In the early sixties, football may have permitted the greatest expression of non-conformity among Soviet people – sportsmen and women were, for example, the only citizens granted an exit visa without having to prove their political loyalty – but the game was still circumscribed by multiple constraints. There were no reported football scandals and little coverage of matches in the media. Match-day programmes were unavailable in those austere, non-commercial days. An announcer simply ran through the teams, as if he were reading the shipping forecast, but in five seconds flat. On my debut I was introduced to the crowd as Yakov Eeeordahnov, turning James into its original Hebrew Yakov (Jacob), and the Irish Riordan into the Jewish Jordan. It was all the same to me. To my friends I was 'Yakov' or 'Yasha'; to acquaintances I was Yakov Villiamovich (James, son of William).

As an amateur – officially all sportspeople were amateurs, to comply with Olympic regulations – I received not a kopeck for my performance. I didn't even get to retain the No. 5 jersey; we had to hand in our kit immediately after the game. There were no names on the backs of shirts in those days, whether in Russia or England. Only years later was I awarded a Spartak red shirt with its diagonal white line across the front and the letter 'S' in the middle. I keep it hanging up neatly ironed in my cupboard . . . in case the call ever comes again.

Since some readers might wonder what a young Englishman was doing in Russia at the height of the Cold War, let alone being a member of such a strange sect as the British Communist Party, I begin my story with a brief description of how I became a communist. At the time I joined in 1959, it took some courage, some might say foolhardiness, to commit myself to a political party that generated fear and suspicion among many people in Britain, especially the powers that be. It certainly was not a sensible career move.

Notwithstanding, it has to be remembered that for most of the twentieth century communism was a force to be reckoned with in most parts of the globe. At one time, its reach spread over three continents and to a third of the world's population. What is more, Soviet communism claimed to be an alternative and superior system to capitalism, and one destined to triumph over it. In my more optimistic days, I had no doubt it was where the future lay.

Today, some forty-five years later, I am able to write about my time in Moscow, hoping it will be a porthole on a small part of history, shedding light on characters who are now mostly dead. For far too long the Soviet Union, as well as communist parties, earned themselves a reputation for extreme mendacity, unwilling and unable to be open and honest, acting like a medieval secret society.

There is another, more important, reason for writing about my contact with football in the Soviet Union. It reveals a role played by football and footballers that is unique in the history of the game. The aphorism, attributed to the old Liverpool manager Bill Shankly, that football is 'more than a matter of life and death' could find no truer expression anywhere else in the world. Soviet football, as I saw it and understood it, also offered an insight into the power of soccer in a relatively closed and often autocratic society where the need for identity and release found a relatively safe locus in the football stadium.

A note of caution. I cannot claim that my emotional attachment to communism, or Portsmouth Football Club, or Spartak, or nostalgia, will preclude what the seventeenth-century French religious philosopher Pascal called 'reasons of the heart of which reason knows nothing'. I am mindful of the warning from the psychologist D. B. Bromley:

> What we remember is often a seriously distorted version
> of what we originally experienced. We not only forget parts

> of what we knew, we also tend to introduce made-up
> parts and to distort and rearrange the whole pattern
> of our experience.

All I can say is that I am aware of the danger. I've done my best to get my memories right, but it is only fair to pass on the warning. With regard to a few of my acquaintances I concur with Marx on memory, 'I never forget a face, but in your case I'll be glad to make an exception.'

Groucho, not Karl.

On the whole, however, my life was greatly enriched by knowing Russian people in general, and footballers in particular. As Albert Camus once said, 'After many years during which I saw many things, what I know most about morality and the duty of man I owe to sport and learned in the RUA [Racing Universitaire Algerios].'

Though many leagues away from Camus' writing, I would say the same about playing centre-half for Spartak. Football has taught me much and given me many of the happiest moments of my life, which is why I put it in the forefront of this book.

1

ЩAR BOY

I was nearly three when war broke out in September 1939. My earliest memory, however, is of a year earlier when Mum, Dad and I were living together, unhappily, in rented rooms in Portsmouth, where I was born. My parents had met at the aircraft company Airspeed. Mum was a shorthand typist, Dad an engineer – one of the many jobs he had throughout his life, none of which lasted more than a year. His lifelong fondness for fine ales and spirits got the better of a commitment to his career or his family. Even in wartime he avoided permanent soldiering on the grounds that his was a vital occupation, and he meandered about the home front. Not so his father, James 'Kit' Riordan, born in Co. Cork. My paternal grandfather not only served longer than most in the army, he remained loyal to his starting rank of gunner for thirty-four years.

Mum and Dad were ill-matched and split up when I was two years old, after only three years together. Among those early memories are the constant rows that I couldn't understand, but which hurt me greatly. Evidently it is the pain of such memories that imprints them on the mind of a young child. What I only discovered fifty years later, at my mother's funeral, was that she had had a child out of wedlock before she met my father. When he rejected the little girl, Eileen, she was fostered out to a family in Bristol. Sadly, I was never to meet her: she died of cancer a year before Mum died. The 'strangers' at Mum's funeral turned out to be Eileen's children and her husband. It is a sad commentary on the moral climate of the period that my dear mother could never share her secret with us, her other children.

When Mum and Dad divorced, they returned to their respective parents. Dad never remarried, never tried to see me or responded to the letters I wrote once I'd left home. Yet, though I didn't know it, I was kept in touch with his family through my grandfather. At junior school I would often notice a burly figure, with fair, wavy hair parted down the middle, standing by the railings of the George Street playground, watching me play football. This man would often call me over and press a silver threepenny piece or sixpence into my hand. He never once said who he was, though he insisted on calling me 'Jim' (my name is James William), while the rest of the family called me 'Bill', 'Billy' or 'Willy' – after my father. My mother must have known who it was (my grandfather was 'Jim' too), but she never let on.

It would be another twenty-five years before I saw Granddad Riordan again, in 1964. He had given up looking for me once I'd moved to another part of town. My then wife, Annick, a nurse, had met my father's sister, Floss, in hospital, and we were invited to my Uncle Ronnie's pub one Sunday afternoon. There sat my grandfather, looking at me, streams of silent tears rolling down his cheeks. It must have pained him to know that I was a communist, for he was a deferential army patriot whose party piece was to recite Kipling's *Gunga*

Din from start to finish. At our next meeting, in Auntie Floss's house at Christmas, he asked me about my politics. I didn't want to hurt him, but neither did I wish to lie, so I admitted I was a red. He took my hand as if pressing another silver coin in it and said, 'Always stick to what you believe.' A lovely person, a real gentleman; everyone said so. I only wish I could have spent more time with him. He died six months later at the age of seventy-four, while I was far away in Moscow.

My father and I got back together after my granddad's funeral and my return home from Russia in 1965. I can't say our relationship was ever warm; we confined ourselves mainly to outings to the Jolly Taxpayer from where I'd often have to 'help' him home. Condemned to an early death from lung cancer, he lived nine more years – thanks to Gold Label barley wine, he reckoned – and eventually died of hypothermia. Those were the days before central heating when, in winter, especially at night, houses were like freezers. Dad got up for the lav and never made it back to bed.

After my parents split up, Mum and I joined the rest of the family in the large Smith household two streets away on the eve of the Second World War. That made eight of us in the two-bedroom terraced house: Mum's four sisters, Granddad and Grandma Smith, my mother and me. Luckily, Uncles George and Harold had married and left home. Our cramped living space was nothing too uncommon in those days, when most working-class families couldn't afford to buy their own home. With Gran sick in the front room, the family crowded into the cosy parlour, with cooking, washing and laundry all done in the tiny floor-tiled scullery which housed the sink and the copper boiler. There was also a small pantry which, facing north, was as good as a fridge in winter. The scullery led into the garden. Outside the back door were the mangle and the rain barrel standing before the corrugated Anderson air-raid shelter, with the lavatory round the side.

Like most people at the time, we had no central heating, no fridge, no washing machine and no vacuum cleaner. No bathroom either: you washed under the scullery cold tap and had a bath in the zinc tub on the parlour floor; each of us took turns, sitting in the war-regulation five inches of tepid water every Friday evening. No kitchen, no indoor lavatory and no electric lighting. Like the streets outside, we had gas lamps. In autumn and winter, it being wartime, we had to pull down the blinds on all the windows from 6.30 p.m. to 6.30 a.m., so that Jerry couldn't spot us in the blackout.

I slept in a bed with three aunts – Rose, Doris and Edie – 'tops to tails': two up one way, two up the other. The bed, not a double by any means, had a grey steel head and foot, a lumpy flock mattress on which I sometimes peed (to my shame and others' discomfort), and large springs that sighed and groaned whenever someone turned over. Under the bed was the common 'gezzunder' (so called because it 'goes under' the bed) in which we did our number ones, and sometimes our number twos, rather than traipsing downstairs and out into the back-garden lav.

On the streets, motorcars, bikes and trams jostled with horses and carts, with stone troughs providing water for thirsty muzzles. Our road saw plenty of horses – drawing milk and coal carts – and hand barrows containing bread, ice cream and, on one occasion a performing monkey. A rag-and-bone man used to trundle his cart through the streets, shouting out RAG-G-G-BO-O-O-NN! He'd give you a couple of pennies for your old stuff or a goldfish in a jamjar. My job was to collect steaming horse manure from the street with a shovel for our back garden vegetables and marigolds.

Soon wartime left the main streets half empty, with most civilian cars kept for emergencies only, especially as petrol, like everything else, was rationed. My mates and I would play out in the empty road: skipping, leap-frog, knucklebones, whipping tops, marbles in the gutters, cricket against the lamp-posts and, my best sport, jumping over dustbins.

It was just before midday on Sunday 3 September 1939 when Granddad Smith switched on the wireless. He had ordered the entire family to be present. Even Grandma, who spent most of her time confined to the sofa-bed in the chilly front room (she was dying of stomach cancer; there were no painkillers to dull the pain), had to drag herself along the passage into the parlour. We all crammed into the small room under a print of the glaring Lord Kitchener ('Your Country Needs You!'), that loomed large on the wall. As ever, Granddad was in his armchair, a blackened cap covering his bald head, with ginger tufts sticking out the side and back. His nicotine-stained fingers were lighting up yet another Woodbine, a 'coffin nail' as we called them. No one dared speak.

All at once, a crackle and hiss issued from the wireless and a grave voice told us that the Prime Minister, Neville Chamberlain, had an important message for us. A cough and clearing of his throat, then it came:

'Grave news . . . given Hitler an ultimatum . . . expired at noon today, the third of September 1939 . . . Mr Hitler has not met our conditions . . . Consequently . . . *we are at war with Germany.*'

Granddad switched it off immediately. No one knew what to say. Perhaps it was the innocence of childhood (I was two years, eleven months old), but I dared to ask, 'What's war?' The silence was almost deafening. All eyes turned to Granddad. He had been a soldier in the Great War, in the Irish

Guards. Invalided out in 1917, he still nursed a wheezy chest from the mustard gas attacks. He never talked about it. Now he wheezed, spat into a dirty handkerchief and cleared his throat. His low growl startled us:

'Hell!'

We were shocked. Granddad didn't allow blasphemy in the house. He was a taciturn tyrant who made sure his word was law: he opened all letters, turned the wireless on and off, switched off the gaslight and decided what time everyone went to bed. He was a chimney sweep by trade and would trundle his black spikey brushes down the passage and through the parlour out into the garden shed every morning, noon and night. All evening long, he would sit in the same armchair, the wrinkles in his forehead indelibly blackened with soot. His was the only black face I ever saw until a few years after the war when the Jamaican winger Lindy Delapenha played in Portsmouth's Golden Jubilee year of 1948–9.

Although Granddad decided what wireless programmes to listen to, there was not much choice in wartime. For economic reasons, the BBC reduced its services to a single station, the Home Service, which provided the news, plays, religious services, educational talks (from the Radio Doctor), and classical and light music (Victor Silvester playing dance music – waltz, quickstep and foxtrot). If any one person was responsible for sowing the seeds of rebellion in me, it was Granddad George Smith. Not only did I think the way he treated us all was unfair, particularly his poor wife (who had run away from him once, with all eight children – one died in infancy; another, Freddie, died in an Army brawl), but I felt an instinctive opposition to all he stood for: King and Country, rigid religious discipline, and a Victorian (he was born in the middle of Victoria's reign) patriarchal tyranny that kept us all in thrall to this soot-black Captain Mainwaring of the chimney stacks.

In wartime, life and death turned on the wheel of fortune. As Portsmouth was such an important naval base, the Jerries dropped bombs on us every night: depots, railway lines, football stadiums, ship wharves or terraced houses, no matter what the target was we all got walloped. The authorities did their bit to protect us, I suppose. Each house had a government-issue Anderson air-raid shelter in the back garden and each street had its Static Water Station (SWS) for dousing German incendiary bombs. We children *knew* that Jerry bombs had English names chalked onto them. If yours was on one that night, it didn't matter what prayers you said or where you hid: it would get you.

One Sunday morning in late August 1941, Mum and I set off for my great-aunt's house on Queen Street, near the Dockyard. We were almost there, passing under the railway bridge into St George's Square – a stone's throw from where the engineer Isambard Kingdom Brunel was born – when the air-raid siren sounded. We had to scuttle for safety into an underground shelter in the middle of the cobblestoned square. There were some sixty old men, women and kids sitting on the wooden bench round the wall, all greeny-pale faces in the dim light of a paraffin lamp. 'That dockyard's in for a right pasting again,' muttered an old fellow huddled up in a muffler and overcoat.

But the Jerry bomber missed the target and dropped his bomb right on our shelter! I can still see, hear, smell and feel it now: screams, smoke, flames, glimpses of daylight through a jagged hole in the roof, a terrific blast of hot air. Luckily for Mum and me, the bomb landed on the poor souls sitting at the other end of the shelter. It must have had their names on it. We were fortunate to escape with no more than shock and singed hair.

Painful memories can act strangely: for fifty years I locked that trauma away in a recess of my mind. One day, I was walking along a road near my house when I passed a building that was being demolished; the smell and the taste of the brick dust on my lips unlocked that recess in my brain and all the horrors came tumbling out. I put them into my very first novel, *Sweet Clarinet*, a children's story about a wartime raid that to my astonishment, won a national award.

Because of the war almost everything was rationed: food, clothing, fuel for heating or cooking, paper (at my first school we used chalk on slates instead of ink on paper) and, worst of all, sweets. I was allowed a paper bagful – four ounces – a week. My favourites were the enormous gobstoppers that changed colour as you sucked them. I'd pass one on to my pals, mouth to mouth, strictly thirty seconds each. Since two or three gobstoppers were a week's ration, we had to pool our resources! Coupons in your ration book entitled you to food, but you had to queue for bread, meat and just about everything else. Mind you, no amount of coupons could earn you oranges and lemons, bananas and pineapples, chocolate or lemonade. As far as we kids were concerned, they did not exist. But we did have powdered eggs that tasted of burnt rubber, blubbery whale meat, oily bloaters and bitter Camp coffee from a bottle. The rationing continued right up until I was eighteen, in 1954. The government did its best to keep up children's strength by issuing free bottles of thick, sweet orange juice, horrid cod liver oil and one third of a pint bottle of milk a day. We supplemented this meagre diet by scrumping apples and gathering blackberries in the autumn, eating mouldy bread with dripping, sucking penny OXO cubes and chewing hawthorn leaves which we called bread and cheese.

Occasionally there were surprises. Thanks to my Auntie Edie, who worked as a nurse on Africa's Gold Coast, I once received the prized possession of a leather football with a real rubber bladder (there were none to be had in the shops for love, money or coupons) that she had sent all the way from Africa.

Just when it stopped raining bombs, in mid-1943, the government in its wisdom decided that we kids would be safer out of town. I did not want to be evacuated. I cried and stamped my feet, even threatened to run away. 'Government orders,' said Mum. She was always blaming the government when difficult decisions had to be made.

So one day in March I was dressed in my Sunday best, handed margarine and plum jam sandwiches, and a piece of cardboard with my name on it was pinned to my jacket. Last but not least, my hated gasmask was slung round my neck. Mum took me by trolley bus to Portsmouth Station where I joined a swirling stream of other evacuees, some, like me, crying their eyes out, some looking lost and miserable, others chattering away like excited monkeys. I was dispatched to a big house in Looe, Cornwall. The train journey seemed to take all day. No doubt it was a nice enough place and those running it did their best for the dozen or more misplaced 'orphans'– they got money and extra coupons as a reward for looking after us – but I have never been so miserable. I remember little of my time there except, oddly, the squawking of seagulls and my own squinnying. If anything marked me for life, it was evacuation. It turned me into a distrustful, insecure loner. It wasn't the family's fault – I just missed my mum. Although I was moved closer to home after a year, to Nutbourne, near Emsworth (on the border of Hampshire and

West Sussex), my misery and loneliness continued right up to late 1944 when I was finally brought home. No prisoner could have been more relieved at getting out of gaol – after a sentence of two years and two months.

Mum had remarried just before the end of the war, having advertised in the local paper for a man, as the moral climate put it, 'with a view to marriage'. What with the dislocation and casualties, such advertisements were common. I suppose the legal tag 'with a view to marriage' was intended to warn off good-time girls/boys from seeking a bit on the side.

Mum's new husband was a quiet, kind man called Ron Brown. This tall, slim, balding 'dockie' was so shy and tongue-tied that he could never have chatted up a prospective bride, even with a drop of Dutch courage. Besides, one pint of brown and mild would make him sick. Before the war Ron had served a five-year apprenticeship in the foundry of Portsmouth Dockyard. During this period, he combined this trade with that of a part-time fireman. His was a regular routine: wash, shave, cut cheese sandwiches the night before, then up at six thirty, cycle to work, return home for half an hour at lunchtime, cycle back to work until five, six days a week (Saturday till midday). He did this for forty-nine years, from the age of fourteen to sixty-four, when he retired in 1971 with a dicky heart – like most men of that era, he smoked heavily.

Ron accepted me as if I was his own son. His spare-time pleasures were confined to betting a few shillings on the horses, watching football and all-in wrestling, and making the occasional trip to dog racing at Portsmouth's greyhound stadium (it still exists). Now and then he took me to the Theatre Royal to watch music hall: the Crazy Gang, Max Miller, Anne Shelton, even Laurel and Hardy once. For me that was magic, as were the flicks on Saturday mornings: I remember the characters, Old Mother Riley, Hopalong Cassidy, Roy Rogers, and the serials which always ended on a huge cliffhanger, so that you had to go back the next week to see what happened.

Poor old Ron could not adjust to retirement. He grew so fat that he had to wrap an overcoat round him (he could no longer do up his trousers) to walk down the road to the bookies. His routine of earlier years fell by the wayside: he rarely washed or shaved, and even stopped going to bed at night, watching TV until the little white dot appeared, then dossing down on the sofa. Eventually he died of a massive heart attack two years after retiring.

When I finally returned from evacuation in 1944, however, I joined Mum, Ron and their new baby, Marilyn, in a rented house. To pay the rent Mum worked as a cleaner, as she did for most of her life, even though her intelligence and short-hand-typing skills suited her for superior employment. Nowadays she'd probably have been a teacher or social worker. Although I feel embarrassed to say it, I look back on the war years in Portsmouth as great fun, one of the happiest periods of my life, blighted only by the difficult period of evacuation. However, at the age of nine, I was about to meet the love of my life – football.

2

THE BEAUTIFUL
RUSSIAN GAME

On Boxing Day 1944, 'Uncle' George (who married Auntie Rose after her first husband, Sid, had gone down with his torpedoed ship, HMS *Barham*, in 1941), a jolly sailor from Aberdeen, took me to Fratton Park, home of Portsmouth Football Club to watch them play Crystal Palace. I was eight at the time and perched uncomfortably on the bar of a crush barrier. During the war, the Football Association had sanctioned three regional competitions: north, south and west, to avoid clubs being involved in long-distance travelling. The year 1944 was significant for Portsmouth in that the manager, Jack Tinn, completed twenty-five years in management, seventeen of them at Fratton Park. At the same time, war hero General Montgomery ('Monty') was elected president of the club.

Portsmouth, like most teams at the time, had many first-team players serving overseas and tried to balance the side with young local lads and 'guest' players stationed in the city. A few of the 1939 cup-winning squad remained: goalkeeper

Harry Walker, full backs Lew Morgan and Bill Rochford, captain Jimmy Guthrie, winger Cliff Parker, inside-forward Bert Barlow and centre-forward Jock Anderson. Then there were three local youngsters vying for a place in the team: Peter Harris, Jimmy Dickinson (who would ultimately become one of Portsmouth's finest players) and Reg Flewin. On this particular day Pompey also had the services of two 'guest' players, both England internationals, Bury's Reg Halton and Arsenal's famous centre-forward and Hampshire lad Ted Drake. The home side ran out easy winners, 9–1, with Ted Drake scoring four. Though it was more than sixty years ago, I still remember him cracking the ball into the net, retrieving it and carrying it to the centre spot, eager to score more. Although wartime restrictions confined the gate to just over 13,000, the atmosphere was so passionate that for me it beat wireless, music hall and the flicks put together. I was hooked. There cannot be many fans whose very first game ended in a 9–1 victory!

After that day out with Uncle George, I started going to Fratton Park on my own, sitting on the white-painted wall at the front of the terraces for the rest of the season. I witnessed no more cricket scores, but I did cheer home wins against Southampton, Aldershot and Fulham, as well as seeing defeats by West Ham, Queens Park Rangers, Millwall and, most shamefully, 0–8 to Brighton, our neighbours on the Sussex coast.

After the war was over, and the regular season resumed, the glory years for Portsmouth FC began. They were high times to be a fan. We were to become one of the greatest teams – if not *the* greatest – in the world. Pompey were full of exciting players and we won the First Division two years running, from 1948 to 1950. I can see them now in their royal blue shirts, baggy white shorts and red socks: Ernie Butler (in green jumper) in goal, Phil Rookes and Harry Ferrier at full-back, Reg Flewin centre-half, Jimmy Dickinson and Jimmy Scoular at wing-half, Peter Harris on the right wing, Jack Froggatt on the left, Dougie Reid and Len Phillips at inside-forward, and Ike Clarke centre-forward. Heroes all. The Christian names alone tell much of their working-class backgrounds and allegiances, Jimmy and Ernie, Harry and Dougie: they were just like us, talked like us, dressed like us, even lived in the same terraced streets as us.

I was convinced that their success was due to me kneeling beside my bed each Friday night, putting my hands together and praying to God to let Pompey win the following afternoon. For two years it worked. As such, there was no more zealous member of Sunday School and the all-boy church choir.

More than 40,000 fans regularly paid sixpence to see the team play in those days. On my twelfth birthday, 10 October 1948, a record 46,327 saw Pompey top the league with a 1–0 win over Newcastle. Such was the fans' zeal that queues started to form at 9.30 that morning (for a three o'clock kick-off), and the crowd 'packers' (the stewards of their day) had their hands full keeping gangways clear. It is a chastening thought that today, thanks to all-seater stadiums, and the fact that Fratton Park has never really been redeveloped, more or less the same ground holds fewer than half that number.

As a rule, I arrived two or three hours early, entertained by the Fire Brigade band marching up and down the pitch, the leader twirling his silver mace and tossing it high into the air (I hoped he'd drop it!). On occasion, I waited for my stepfather Ron to finish work and have his dinner; like all dock workers he did a five-and-a-half-day week – half a day less than professional footballers. If ever I arrived at the ground late, men would pass me over their heads down to the perimeter wall where I'd sit, reading my penny programme. At half-time a man high on a platform behind one goal fitted half-time scores onto the scoreboard, rather as they put up cricket scores today at old grounds.

Post-war Britain was ravaged by bombed sites and skeletons of buildings, and there were massive shortages. It took hundreds of coupons to rig out a football team, with fans often donating their own clothing coupons. To this day, a friend boasts of his granddad, 'Zigger' Holmes, a pig farmer on the Isle of Wight, sending his entire allocation in response to the club's appeal for five hundred clothing coupons to buy shirts for the team. With rubber supplies cut off, footballs were also hard to come by (putting that earlier present from Auntie Edie into sharp perspective). No luxury in those days of using a different ball for each game. Clubs had no Tannoy systems either, so a man would carry a blackboard on a pole round the ground with team changes chalked on it. He was followed by a seller of 'cough-no-more' sweets laid on a tray before him.

Some players were still abroad and those available were earning the average pre-war wage of £4 a week, with only the stars like Lawton, Drake, Matthews, Mortensen, Raich Carter and Alex James taking home the princely sum of £8 a week. So hard up were footballers that the Players' Union called the first-ever strike in November 1945. And footballers weren't alone in their new-found militancy: across the country homecoming servicemen expected a 'land fit for heroes' and were determined to prevent a return to the austere and exploitative thirties. It was this prevailing mood that had ditched Winston Churchill's Conservative Party in favour of Clement Attlee's

Labour Party in the shock 1945 election result. The pre-war Portsmouth captain, Jimmy Guthrie, who had led the team to a 4–1 victory in the 1939 Cup Final against Wolverhampton Wanderers, left the club in 1946, having been elected chairman of the Professional Footballers' Association. He campaigned hard for players' rights, gained grudging success and was later to join the Communist Party – I once bumped into him at a *Daily Worker* rally in London's Albert Hall.

Although I was only nine when the war ended, one event occurred that, I feel sure, had a big influence on my lifelong love affair with Russia. Moscow Dinamo came to Britain in the autumn of 1945. It was not necessarily the best Soviet team, having lost the Cup Final 1–0 just three weeks earlier to the Central Army Sports Club but it was funded by the security services and its loyalty to the Soviet authorities made it an ideal and trustworthy candidate for their first sports envoy.

I remember listening eagerly to the crackly acid-battery wireless set as the first Russian team to visit us, and also the first Soviet team to tour the West, flew into Croydon Airport. Dinamo arrived on a wave of popular goodwill and respect thanks to the decisive Red Army contribution to the Allied victory. Few British people then knew anything about the nature of the Soviet regime, the purges, the labour camps or the character of Stalin and his secret police chief, Lavrenty Beria. That would all come later.

Most of the journalistic comment about Moscow Dinamo in the British press was embarrassingly ignorant. What the newspapers didn't know they made up. For example, it was generally claimed that the 'cheating' Russians had sent a composite team of the best Soviet players, a sort of national squad. In fact, if they had been able to read Russian, journalists would have discovered that the Dinamo team which had been beaten in the Cup Final was, with one exception, precisely the one that arrived at Croydon Airport. That exception was the centre-forward Vsevolod Bobrov, a member of the army side (who also played ice hockey), who had been transferred to Dinamo for the tour.

On the other hand, apart from the communist *Daily Worker*, virtually no national daily mentioned that Dinamo's first opponents, Chelsea, had just bought inside-forward Len Goulden, centre-half John Harris and England's regular centre-forward Tommy Lawton (transferred from Everton for the then record sum of £14,000). If that were not enough, Chelsea had also drafted in two guests from Fulham, Jim Taylor, an England international left-half, and Joe Bacuzzi, the England left-back. The match was played at Stamford Bridge, which had escaped the Blitz virtually unscathed.

For reasons of austerity (and perhaps because football was the workers' game, in contrast to tennis, cricket and the Oxford v. Cambridge Boat Race), the BBC's Raymond Glendenning commentated only on the second half. I eagerly listened in, my ear literally pressed to the wireless set. It being a Tuesday afternoon, Granddad was at work, so I had the wireless to myself. We were lucky to get even that as the Cup Final was normally the only football match broadcast during the year. Like all BBC broadcasters of the period, sports commentators spoke with plummy, upper-class voices, whether on boxing, football, horse racing or cricket. No regional accents were permitted, thereby reinforcing the 'superiority' of the ruling class. So with Glendenning.

At half-time, Chelsea were undeservedly leading 2–0. But in an exciting second half, Chelsea scored once more from a

Tommy Lawton trademark header, and Dinamo put three goals past the Chelsea keeper, Woodley; Bobrov equalized with five minutes to go. So the game ended 3–3, and the crowd (some say it was 100,000) poured onto the pitch, hoisted the Russians on their shoulders and carried them from the field as if they were conquering heroes.

So the Russians could play a bit. 'The greatest club side to visit this island,' wrote L. V. Manning in the *Daily Sketch*. Perhaps the draw had been a fluke? A few days later, the 'massacre' of Cardiff at Ninian Park, 10–1, laid that idea to rest.

Since the next match, against Arsenal (but played at White Hart Lane in thick fog), was such a prestigious event (this was getting beyond a joke! English pride was at stake), the FA decided to 'reinforce' the home side with 'guest' players: Stanley Matthews from Stoke, Stan Mortensen from Blackpool, Cardiff's goalkeeper Wyn Griffiths, Fulham's Joe Bacuzzi (again) and Ronnie Rooke, and Bury's Reg Halton. As a result, most of those who played in Arsenal shirts were not Arsenal players at all (many were still serving abroad), but star footballers brought in from other clubs. The Dinamo captain, Semichastny, did say after the match that the list of Arsenal players originally submitted was not the one he had received just prior to the match, and that the Arsenal team was in effect not a club team at all, but a representative one. As it turned out, it made no difference: Dinamo won a tightly contested game 4–3. That victory, on the Wednesday, really made people sit up and take notice. Perhaps English football was not the best in the world, after all? The crushing answer to that was to come eight years later when the Hungarians arrived and walloped England 6–3, then won the return match 7–1.

The Dinamo tour was rounded off with a 2–2 draw at Ibrox Stadium against Glasgow Rangers – by far the most successful pre- and immediate post-war Scottish side. The Russian coach, Mikhail Yakushin, unintentionally poked the English in the eye by remarking that the Scots were the fittest and finest footballers his team had met in Britain. So Dinamo remained unbeaten, and I followed all their games in the papers. They returned home to a heroes' welcome.

The British tour seemed to promise closer and friendlier relations between the Soviets and the West, yet the imminent Cold War was to have a lasting, prohibitive impact on future Soviet contacts with foreign states. We would see no more Russians playing in Britain for many years to come. Ironically, it was precisely this burgeoning international tension that was to force Russian upon me in National Service and bring me into contact with Russians.

As for British football, the Russians had taught us some valuable lessons. Not only had they demonstrated a tactical revolution in style of play, they had shown several other innovations worth taking up: pre-match warm-ups, substitutions, a different interpretation of the rules (no barging the goalkeeper into the net or kicking the ball out of his hands). But, generally speaking, the wake-up call to British football went unheeded. Visiting foreign teams continued to provide reminders that football in the British Isles lacked tactical ingenuity and basic skills, put too much emphasis on speed and strength, and not enough on skill and finesse.

In the meantime, my own football skills were being polished by kicking a bald tennis ball against brick walls to and from school, hitting targets hour after hour in our back alley, and taking part in playground kickabouts. We were still living in the rented terraced house, two pubs and a church away from my school. Since I towered over my schoolmates, even at nine, I played centre-half in the school team with boys two years older than me. The biggest threat to my progress was that I was the only one without football boots. With three other children to clothe – Marilyn, Terry (born in September 1946) and Jennifer (she was Mum's 'little afterthought') – Mum was too poor to buy luxuries like leather football boots. Inevitably the soles of my shoes were always full of holes, patched over with bits of cardboard. So I played either in an old pair of black plimsolls or my stepfather's carpet slippers held together with rubber bands. There were compensations perhaps: I learned to pass more accurately, to kick harder with my instep instead of giving the ball a toe poke, to trap and control the ball. When I was ten, the junior school team, George Street, reached the cup final, to be played at our own 'Wembley', Fratton Park. The school sports teacher, Mr Hearn, who had lost a leg in the war, had a whip-round in the staffroom for money and coupons to buy me my first pair of boots: they were hard-nosed, fawn, smelling intoxicatingly of leather and dubbin. Now, with real boots, I'd surely be transformed into Tommy Lawton or Ted Drake. Alas, I just couldn't get used to them, partly because they were too big, but mostly because I was used to my shabbier footwear. We drew the final and lost the replay.

It took nearly a year to grow into the new boots. I was looking forward to captaining the school side, but Mum, who had wanderlust, moved the family to another part of town, Tipner, near the greyhound stadium; this meant a new school. When my new headmaster asked what I wanted to be when I grew up, I rashly said 'footballer'. Possibly to cure me of this undesirable and impoverished ambition, he stuck me in goal, where I was worse than useless, boots or no boots.

Within a year, Mum grew tired of our new house and we were off again, this time due south to Southsea, a salubrious part of town, close to the beach. The new rented house had three bedrooms and an attic, and so could be let to holidaymakers in the summer while we slept in the stifling attic. Those were the days when British workers looked no further than Sunny Southsea, Skegness, Blackpool or one of Billy Butlin's holiday camps for their fortnight's summer break.

At my new school, Albert Road Juniors, I took the exam that was to determine my and everyone else's future (except the small percentage of the population rich enough to pay for private schooling): the eleven-plus. Those who 'failed' it (80 per cent) went to a secondary modern school to become manual workers; the next 5 per cent of boys went to a technical or building school, while the top 15 per cent went to a state grammar school where boys and girls studied separately. The grammar schools were run along the lines of public schools, with houses, prefects (who wore braided jackets), streaming and the ultimate ambition of preparing the elite for entry to Oxford or Cambridge. In truth, in my school most rose no higher than five-year apprenticeships in Portsmouth Dockyard as coppersmiths, riveters and electricians.

To the incomprehension of most of my relatives, 'our Billy' passed the exam and got kitted out (on Provident savings coupons) for Portsmouth Southern Grammar School for Boys. Since my new school was in Southsea, just along Albert Road from my junior school, I had no more than a mile to walk from home. So close was it to the beach that in summer we spent our PE lessons swimming in the sea.

By now we'd moved from slates to pen-nibs dipped in inkwells – the new-fangled biros were banned for fear of them disfiguring our handwriting. We all sat at double wooden desks with iron frames; the windows were too high for us to be distracted by looking out, and the walls were of dark brown glazed tiles. In winter we had open fires close to which were placed the free one-third milk bottles to thaw out the milk.

One activity my new school encouraged was reading. Being a bit of a misfit (perhaps because of my early fatherless status, evacuation to the West Country and war-trauma experience, and our relative poverty), I took to reading like a duck to water, devouring the children's books that were popular in the late forties. Although I enjoyed being taken away to desert islands with Robinson Crusoe, and discovering King Solomon's mines with Allan Quatermain, I could not help wondering about the near total absence of the people I lived among in what I read. Public schoolboys were everywhere (from Tom Brown to Billy Bunter), along with the middle-class kids of Enid Blyton, C. S. Lewis, J. M. Barrie, Anna Sewell and the rest. So were officers like Biggles and Worrals, squires and colonial types as portrayed by Kipling and Robert Louis Stevenson. Ordinary working people, black people, gypsies and other 'undesirables' hardly got a look in. If they did feature they were often portrayed as stupid, uncouth and cruel, like workers transmogrified as stoats and weasels in (Bank of England Secretary) Kenneth Grahame's *The Wind in the Willows*.

To tell the truth, it hardly occurred to me then how arrogant and racist such books were. Perhaps for that reason my favourites were comics where a few 'real' people mixed it with the toffs. With the five shillings a week I earned from my paper round (which I did for over two years, seven days a week), I purchased *Wizard* and *Eagle*, and read several others, such as *Rover*. In them I could follow the football adventures of Cannonball Kid as well as other 'common' sporting heroes, like Alf Tupper – 'Tough of the Track' (who delighted in beating 'snooty, toffee-nosed types' and thrived on a diet of fish and chips), Wilson the Wonder Man and the jockey Tim Duggan. Few of our 'superiors' realized then how subversive these comics actually were.

Since my grammar school was run by a martinet head, Henry Mills, steeped in public school values, it believed implicitly in team games as integral to character training. Besides coldish showers and the obligatory annual long-distance slog (still in my carpet slippers) up and down Portsdown Hill which hems in the city, we enjoyed plenty of football and cricket – for house, year and school. Thankfully, I was restored to centre-half where I didn't have to run fast, pass accurately or jump high. Though possessing bags of enthusiasm, alas I never excelled or got selected for any representative team outside school (except, to my embarrass-ment, the rifle shooting team of our Combined Cadet Force).

In 1953 I gained the requisite four 'A' levels demanded by universities at the time (Latin, French, German and Econom-ics, along with 'O' level Maths and English which I had passed earlier). Since none of my family spoke a foreign language, I can only put my linguistic facility down to hard work and cramming. Despite my four 'A's (albeit with moderate grades) and two 'O's, I had no intention of going to university. I could not turn my back on my mates and family. Although the Labour government had opened up universities by providing grants for working-class boys and girls to study, post-war England was still a strongly class-ridden society. Class governed everything and identified you everywhere: the sports you played and followed, the clothes you wore, the way you spoke, the jobs you aspired to and took, the street you lived in, the rank you took in the armed forces. To desert your class was a bold and, to many people, disloyal step. My mother sometimes told me how much nagging she had to put up with from uncles and neighbours in my last year at school. 'Isn't it time Billy was bringing in money?' 'All that studying will make him go blind.' 'He'll end up becoming one of them [i.e. the "other" class].' It took a lot of courage for her to resist; perhaps her own confined life made her determined to support my chance to broaden my horizons (she even took an evening job as a barmaid to help me improve my maths and Latin). Looking back, I realize that class prejudice was as much ingrained in the working class as it was in the rich and privileged. At the time, I was prepared to study, but not yet ready to pull up my roots.

My schooldays were generally happy and rewarding. So much so that today, in my seventies, I regularly meet old schoolfriends to chat over 'the good old days': Johnner Lee, Frank 'Pimple' Harfield, Chas Foreman, 'Stan the Man' Brian Stanley, Terry Wheeler, Ted 'Whistler' Forehead, Stu Denyer, Derek 'Spike' Thomas and many more from Jim 'Lofty' Riordan's year and team. Even our old physics master, Ian 'Willy' Watson, comes along to our get-togethers. And we still call him 'Sir'.

3

THE DARTMOOR RUSSKI

Like nearly all my school pals, I had my immediate future mapped out for me after school: two years' National Service. Unless medically unfit, every young man had to do his duty to Queen and Country. Between school, which I left the moment I could, in June 1953, and the forces, for which I enlisted in March 1954, I did a range of jobs to bring money into the household: hotel boot boy, dance band musician (double bass), postman, railway enquiries clerk, and crate stacker at Portsmouth and Brighton United Brewery. The last-named entailed stacking wooden crates filled with a dozen pint bottles of beer. It was a job I firmly intended taking up again on demob, even if it found little use for Latin, French or German. In spite of my school results, I never considered myself brainy, certainly not ambitious. To pursue any ambitions beyond manual work meant taking the huge step of deserting my class. At the brewery not only was I a champion stacker, piling up as many as fourteen at a time, I was among my own. Outside school, the only people I had ever known were working class. The brewery trade satisfied my social and class conscience and the expectations of immediate family (apart from Mum) and it avoided the uncertainty of leaving home, meeting people who spoke differently and might look down on an ignoramus like me. Here, the smells and sounds, the overalls and bikes, the fags and beer, music and robust language were all cosily familiar.

When signing-on day dawned, in March 1954, my natural choice as a Portsmouth boy – the Royal Navy – would not have me because the only available jobs were in the galley – and you had to be a near midget to qualify. That left the RAF and the Army. Since the 'pongos' (Army) sounded too much like hard grind, I plumped for the 'Brylcreem Boys' of the RAF; which seemed altogether more civilized. After being kitted out at Cardington, in Bedfordshire, losing my Teddy Boy quiff and DA ('Duck's Arse' or 'District Attorney' – take your pick), and spending my first night away from home since evacuation (as were most of my companions, judging from the snuffles from neighbouring beds once the lights went out), I was sent to RAF Hednesford in the Black Country for eight weeks of 'square-bashing'. Now began the most frightening time of my life. Some thirty of us neophytes from all over the country lived cheek by jowl in a long wooden hut. Like prisoners, we were not allowed out of the camp. Our comradeship – we were thrown together by dint of being in the same stew – helped see us through this hell on earth. And hell is what it was intended to be.

The purpose of square-bashing is to break and re-form you into an unthinking automaton. If you don't submit, your life is made a misery. Reveille at 6.30 to screams from your hut commandant, beating a cricket stump – rat-a-tat-tat-tat – on the iron bed rails. Polish your brasses and boots till Corporal can see his face in them. Blanco your belt. Square off your blankets and pillow at the head of the bed. Scrub and polish the floor – don't walk on it, slide along on polishing rags. Keep your locker tidy. Nothing here is private or personal. Always address the Corporal as 'Corporal': 'Yes, Corporal.' 'No, Corporal.' Do your ablutions in the washhouse by 7.30. Breakfast in the canteen, using 'irons' (cutlery) with your number stamped on them.

On the barrack square for drill at eight o'clock. Square up shoulder to shoulder, with the tallest (me) at the end as right marker. Inspection. Stand to attention. Now drill can commence. Quick march. Left turn. Right turn. About turn. Mark time. 'You stupid little man!' When you've mastered left from right, you can go on to rifle drill. Don't for heaven's sake drop the damn thing! And so on, all day long. All week long. All month long.

The lesson I learned was salutary, and it stayed with me for the rest of my life. Put young men into an alien environment and, with methods of fear and disorientation, you can break and turn them into unthinking soldiers who obey commands without hesitation: hate, torture, stick a bayonet into someone's guts, shoot his head off. Not all succumbed. Rumour had it that three young men committed suicide, one by drinking two tins of Brasso. I like to think I retained a free zone in my brain, while my body carried out orders. Open resistance was futile. Sent to the guardhouse for not saluting an officer, I spent hours on my knees washing and polishing the floor. When I asked if that was all, the guard, without looking round, tossed the remains of his mug of tea over my spotless floor. 'Do it again!' I came to hate all officers – public school boys to a man – and the skivvies who did their dirty work. Those civilians who today call for the reintroduction of National Service to discipline young people have no idea of the reality of such mental cruelty and its brutalizing consequences.

At the end of this 'brainwashing' process, I was allocated a trade and a posting: cook, second class, West Hartlepool. No explanation. That's simply what happened. No asking if that's what I wanted to do or what I was good at. Then, to my surprise, a telegram arrived the day before I was due to depart for the frozen north, re-routing me to Bodmin in Cornwall. For what, the telegram didn't say. Presumably it was none of my business.

When the steam train wheezed into Bodmin Station (the end of the line), in June 1954, I noticed some strange letters painted in black on a hut roof: *MYACHI*, which I later found out was the Russian for 'balls'. Not the testicular variety (that translates as 'eggs'), though the student of Russian obviously had not got that far in his studies. I was also surprised to see the weirdest group of soldiers, airmen and sailors imaginable: casual, superior, unsoldierly in the extreme. Clearly untameable.

Welcome to the Joint Services School for Linguists.

Looking back, I can only assume that those vetting future minor spies like me discovered that I had kept my nose clean politically, dutifully carried out my basic training and was evidently good at languages. If someone was watching me, I was too concerned with survival to notice. So I was suitable material for low-level espionage against the Russkies.

It took me fifty-three years to pluck up courage to return to Bodmin. On the barrack wall of the Duke of Cornwall's Light Infantry is a blue plaque, unveiled in 2004 by the RAF Linguists' Association. It reads:

Between 1951 and 1956, the Joint Services School for
Linguists was located at Walker Lines, Bodmin.
Here linguists were trained for covert work, their vigilance
contributing to national security during the Cold War.

I had not chosen to defend my country. I had not opted for National Service. Or Russian. Like most of my service comrades and, I guess, national servicemen the world over, I was obliged by law to do my time, and I was doing so unwillingly. But since I was here, I might as well make the best of it until my 730 days were up. I wasn't to know then that the experience would totally change my life.

I was to become a student of Russian, spending my time in Cornish classrooms rather than crawling on my belly in the jungles of Malaya, in the deserts of Suez and Iraq, under fire in Cyprus, or simply learning to kill the foe with bayonet and rifle on Bodmin Moor. That suited me fine. I hated violence. I'd always avoided school fights, domestic rows and ignored taunts about my height. I'd even baulked at boxing in the school gym. I never worshipped brave British pilots who'd bombed to bits the German cities of Dresden and Hamburg, let alone the US A-bomb destruction of Hiroshima and Nagasaki. Perhaps I was a mummy's boy, but pacifism was in my nature. Come to think of it, my fellow national servicemen were also in no hurry to kill or be killed.

On the whole, we 'war boys' were far from being gung-ho. Having lived through such a terrifying war and Blitz, we craved the quiet life. We didn't harbour any hatred towards foreign countries and their citizens and we were turning against the values of the older generation that had fought the war. This was a process that gathered pace in the late forties and early fifties as the Empire disintegrated and Britain ceased to be a world power. The massive peace movement, with its marches and demonstrations (in which I took part), was an expression of that mood.

But we were not to get the peace we craved. Nor were we given a chance to build on the friendships forged by the war.

This was particularly so in regard to the Red Army, which had done and suffered more than any army to save the world from fascism. Being in hock to the USA through the 'Lend-Lease' agreement meant following their foreign policy, which thanks to the domestic fearmongering of powerful politicians such as Senator McCarthy, had become radically anti-communist in the post-war period That's why I was learning the language of the West's No. 1 enemy. The developing Cold War was increasingly coming to dominate international affairs and propaganda. To be a communist in a capitalist land, or a capitalist in a communist one, was now tantamount to treason.

There was an even better alternative to learning Russian at Bodmin. It was Chinese, the language of Britain's second major enemy in the estimation of our war lords. The top 5 per cent were swiftly creamed off the new Bodmin intake and dispatched to the more salubrious setting of Cambridge University. Not me. I wasn't bright enough for Cambridge or Chinese, so I was stuck with Russian for the next nine months, from early August 1954 to May 1955.

Being in a closed environment, rather like a private boarding school, we students learned Russian easily and swiftly from native Russians. They had us day in, day out, lightening the learning load with Russian songs, films, novels and plays we put on ourselves. Within eight months I had added another 'A' level to my CV, and this time with an A grade.

I soon found out that I was rubbing shoulders with some of Britain's brainiest young men, a few of whom had already completed a university degree. They were also the worst soldiers ever to disgrace a barrack square. Yet they were to become some of the country's brightest luminaries. They included authors and playwrights like Alan Bennett, D. M. Thomas, Dennis Potter and Michael Frayn, future British ambassadors, heads of

Oxbridge colleges, a bishop, a Governor of the Bank of England (Eddie George), a Chairman of ICI (John Harvey-Jones), officers in the Secret Service, and most teachers of Russian in British schools and universities. Not that I or the other eighteen-year-olds had any idea of the glorious future yet to come.

It ought to be recorded that there was never any crude anti-Soviet propaganda from our teachers at Bodmin, despite what some of the exiled Russian teachers must have gone through. At least one was known to have served with the SS, but most were displaced unfortunates. What the native Russian teachers did, however, was implant in us an appreciation of the beauty of the Russian language and literature. Most of the Bodmin linguists whom I later met retained a genuine affection for Russian and our Russian school. As D. M. Thomas, the author of such books as *The White Hotel*, attested, 'It created a generation of young and influential Britons who had generous, respectful and affectionate feelings for Russia – the eternal Russia of Tolstoy, Pushkin and Pasternak.'

And I was no different. As it did for the future generation of novelists and playwrights, my tutelage at Bodmin stoked my curiosity for Soviet culture and literature – of Gorky and Sholokhov, Ostrovsky and Gladkov, Blok and Yesenin. Although my reading was mostly in English – ironically, the books were translated in Moscow, where I was later to work – I took to this new literature with huge enthusiasm: Gorky's wanderings among the down-and-outs, Sholokhov's descriptions of building collective farms, Ostrovsky's tales of his civil war days, Gladkov's wonderfully named novel *Cement*, and Blok's and Yesenin's irreverent poetry, lampooning greedy priests and lauding revolutionary free spirits.

I might not have risen to such dizzy heights as some of my illustrious comrades-in-arms, but at least I could later claim notoriety in having trained for 'covert work' on both sides of the political divide. And none of those governors, bishops, ambassadors or professors ever played football for Moscow Spartak!

4

OИЩAЯDS AИD ЦРЩAЯDS

One advantage of the armed services was that they catered more for physical than mental development. So football facilities were bountiful in Bodmin. Although our motley crew of effete students of Russian mostly preferred listening to jazz or classical music rather than having a rough and tumble on the football pitch, the neighbouring Cornish light infantrymen were always up for a game. They included talented young players on the books of West Country teams such as Plymouth, Exeter, Torquay and the two Bristols, Rovers and City. Being infantrymen they were used to trampling over the enemy, so apart from getting bruised shins and ribs, I learned the art of nudge and barge that was integral to football of the fifties.

Football opportunities expanded when I was posted to Berlin after a year, in August 1955. My home for the next eight months, till March 1956, was to be Gatow, a district of south-western Berlin, once Hitler's elite Luftwaffe training base. It was just down the road from the Olympic Stadium that had held the Nazi Olympics in 1936 (the year I was born) made famous by Jesse Owens' heroics in front of Hitler.

It was here where two years after the Olympics, in 1938, with the British government clinging to its policy of appeasement, England played Germany at Berlin's Olympic Stadium, with the Football Association (on the orders of the Foreign Office via the British Embassy) demanding that English players give the Nazi salute. Although Hitler was not present, several other Nazi notables were, principally Gestapo chief Hermann Goering and head of Nazi propaganda Josef Goebbels. As Stanley Matthews was to reveal in his memoirs, 'We were appalled. I have never known such an atmosphere in an England dressing room.' Players were the last to be considered.

Notwithstanding the players' reluctance, the team ended up giving the Nazi salute, being unwilling to defy the football and political authorities. It wasn't the first time the pre-war British government showed its true colours. Ten years before, in 1928, the Home Secretary (the reactionary William Joynson-Hicks) had refused entry visas for a Soviet football team from the Don Basin coalfields. He said that he did not want to encourage 'a political approach' to sport. The miners' team had been invited to England after the London Workers' team (a communist outfit led by George Sinfield, London Party official and worker sports enthusiast) had played in six Soviet cities in 1927. The London team lost all its games, one by 11–0 before 35,000 spectators – the priorities of the English and Soviets being patently different. The then Secretary of the Football Association, Sir Frederick Wall, made it clear that the FA would have banned the Russians (and *all* 'continental' teams) in any case. In a classic dollop of humbug, he said,

'Football in dear old England is merely a sporting entertainment . . . England regards international

matches as a game, but Continental countries look upon
these matches as a test of strength, spirit and skill. Victory
increases national prestige, and defeat is a sign of
decadence. To them, success is vital.'

Two years later, when Ivor Montagu, the International Table
Tennis Federation president, tried to arrange a Soviet tour for
West Ham United FC, the Foreign Office advised against it,
claiming that the FO 'could not guarantee repatriation in the
event of the hosts going bankrupt' (!). Of course, the FA
would not consent without Foreign Office approval. So much
for 'no politics in sport', as Montagu commented.

Nearly twenty years after the 'Nazi' Olympics, in 1955,
when I went there, Berlin was situated at the epicentre of the
Cold War. Although the capital of the Soviet-occupied
German Democratic Republic (East Germany) and well
inside the Soviet-ruled third of Germany, the city itself had
been divided into four sectors: British, French, Soviet and
American. Berlin was to be a constant source of friction
between East and West. For us 'sprogs', as we national servicemen were known, the ins and outs of international politics
thankfully flew well over our heads. We couldn't wait to
trample the cobblestones of Hitler's old capital, meet the
fräuleins and even have a chin-wag with the Russian 'enemy'
lurking across the way. For practically all of us, it was our first
venture outside the British Isles. We wouldn't allow ourselves
to be consumed by the officially sanctioned prejudices.

Although the Berlin Wall was not to be built for another
five years, in 1961, movement between East and West Berlin
was nonetheless greatly impeded for civilians by their having
to pass through checkpoints. For us uniformed occupiers,
however, passage to and from sectors was unencumbered.

Thus, I had my first face-to-face meetings with Soviet Russians, even if they were, like me, national servicemen. I thought it quite daring to test my Russian on, and to be photographed with, 'the enemy', especially at the Soviet war memorial at Treptow, featuring a statue of a Russian soldier holding a child and trampling on a broken swastika.

My curiosity about the other side extended to visiting the Soviet bookshop on Potsdamer Platz and buying booklets in English written by Stalin. I certainly couldn't make head or tail of Stalin's *On the Metallurgical Industry* but reading it was more a gesture of defiance than serious interest, like my playing of the Soviet national anthem loudly at midnight, with my radio pointing through the open window at the officers' quarters. I made no bones about my disaffection with the British Establishment and attraction to communism in my letters home to my mum. My communist sympathies stemmed from a mixture of a working-class chip on my shoulder against the officer class and a more general dismay with social injustice, as well as an assumed affinity with Soviet soldiers down the road in Berlin. The way I saw it, I was against the anti-Russian British officers, ergo I had to be for the Russians (though I didn't know any!).

Old schoolfriends to whom I wrote subsequently told me they had been visited by plainclothes police officers, asking questions about me. It is surprising I had no visit myself; perhaps the powers that be thought I'd grow out of such infantile nonsense. They knew that we national servicemen were there under sufferance and most of us had no loyalty to the forces or the anti-Soviet work we had to do. Most were bolshie, in the sense of an awkward and rebellious crew, not Bolshevik sympathizers. If we had been apolitical before, National Service certainly radicalized a great number of us, a mood that was nourished by the general political unrest of the fifties.

My duties at RAF Gatow were far from tedious. After entering a wire cage in the secret section of the base, I had to climb the stairs to sit before a high-powered radio, don earphones, twiddle a few knobs and listen in to other people's conversations. In this instance, the 'other people' were Soviet pilots and ground staff on the other side of the divide, just a few miles away in East Germany. I was supposed to write down the time, code names and all that passed between the two: 'Bullfinch, this is Bullfinch. *Snegir, eto Snegir. Vy menya slushayete?* Are you hearing me? Over.' Time 1103. What British intelligence back in London made of it I never discovered. When we were bored, we tuned into jazz on the American Forces Network instead of Soviet planes. National Service taught me more about Count Basie and Duke Ellington than it ever did about Russian Mig fighters.

And at long last my footballing 'talent' or, rather, my physical attributes as a stopper, were being recognized. After a few games for RAF Gatow in various parts of the British zone of northern Germany, I was selected to play for a team with the grandiloquent title of the British Army on the Rhine (BAOR). The only trouble was we were a bit stuck for opponents. The Americans didn't play proper football. The Russians were out of bounds and, as we were frequently told by higher-ups, a bigger enemy than the defeated Germans (our orders were, in an emergency, to surrender to Germans before Russians). It was hard to get our heads round this. The American playwright Arthur Miller, quoted by John Steinbeck in *A Russian Journal* (1948), expressed the feelings of many of us when he wrote,

> The Germans clearly were to be our new friends, and the
> saviour – Russians – the enemy, an ignoble thing it seemed

> to me . . . this ripping off of Good and Evil labels and
> pasting them onto another.

In any case, the Germans were the conquered foe and therefore unworthy of any game involving fair play. More likely, British Army Command dared not risk humiliating defeat at German hands or, rather, feet.

So we BAOR select few had occasional outings against the only politically acceptable nation left: the French. For the most part, our raggle-taggle bunch of players, captained by a randy Irish corporal called 'Paddy' Flynn (we all knew he was knocking off the sergeant referee's wife), the highest rank among us, was reduced to playing among ourselves, tackling British base teams from Hamburg to Hanover, Cologne to Munster, before a crowd of service personnel and German cleaners. It was all good fun and was later to boost my credentials in Moscow when my Spartak team-mates assumed that the BAOR team was the equivalent of their Central Army Sports Club, TsSKA, a much tidier and professional outfit than we ever were.

I did not go back to the brewery in Portsmouth upon demob in March 1957. During my RAF days I had come across numerous clever dicks who had been to university and their articulacy and knowledge of literature, art and music (especially jazz) convinced me of my need for further education. Before National Service I'd never given a thought to university. Now, my newly expanded horizons made me realize that there was a world beyond stacking beer crates and reading the *Daily Mirror*. I was becoming painfully aware of my ignorance of history, politics and the arts. So every evening, while my mates went off mostly to the NAAFI, I shut myself away in a room to read back issues of *The Economist* (its name deluding me into believing it was apolitical) and various history books.

No one in my family had ever dreamed of going, let alone applied, to university, and it was not easy for my mother to convince doubting relatives yet again why Billy should not now be earning a proper living. Looking back, it's clear she had a sense of my potential for breaking the bonds of working-class culture. I owe her everything.

My mother lived to see me collect my doctorate from Birmingham University – an occasion that brought her and my father together for the first time in thirty-six years – but not to become a professor or children's author, which would have made her very proud. I used to sit by her grave in a Portsmouth cemetery (she is buried with her mother, Mary Smith) to share my latest news, books and university career. I never mentioned football, even though she and I occasionally used to go to watch Pompey together. I wouldn't call her a football fan; like most working-class women she shared men's interests in football, passively. But unlike most women of the time, Mum did stand on the terraces, singing and shouting her support in her strong, shrill Wiltshire tones.

Emotionally, I was radical and rebellious, while I remained politically and culturally illiterate. At home we had been brought up on a diet of the *Daily Mirror* during the week, and the *News of the World* (still broadsheets in those days but with the familiar tabloid leanings) on Sunday. There was the occasional glimpse of pictures and scandals in *Titbits* when I visited the barber's. The only other publications that my schoolboy eye feasted upon were comics and their invariable football stories, *Charles Buchan's Football Monthly* and the naturist *Health & Efficiency* with all the best bits air-brushed out. Mine was a typical 'retarded' teenage experience of the 1950s: no page three nudes, little pop music permitted on the radio (there was no television) – we had to tune in to Radio Luxembourg for the Top Twenty. Ironically, this straitlaced experience was later to be replicated in Moscow where I had to listen in to the BBC for the latest pop music. Back in fifties Britain, however, there were no clubs or DJs, and certainly no substance abuse, save fags, beer and Babycham. Pubs and dance halls shut down at ten thirty (eleven on Saturdays) so we could get a good night's sleep before the next day's work. For excess energy there was football.

I made vain attempts to get into Oxbridge, the only universities which Mr Mills, my old headmaster, had ever mentioned. I filled in an application form for Selwyn College, Cambridge (only because it sounded small), giving my father's occupation and religion, and sending five guineas. I received a refusal a fortnight later. No explanation. There is no doubt I wasn't cultured enough. Equally, I was not of the right class background. I then lowered my sights and sat an entry examination for the London School of Economics. No luck there either. In the end, after perusing various other university prospectuses, I had to settle for Birmingham and a Russian Studies degree. As it turned out, I could not have made a better choice. Birmingham was the only university in England with a department (the Centre for Russian and East European Studies) devoted to a serious political, economic and social study of the Soviet Union.

I was greatly influenced by my three lecturers, Bob Davies, Geoff Barker and Elizabeth Koutaissov, as well as the Head of the Centre, Professor Alexander Baykov. Baykov had a particularly interesting story. As a young man in Russia he'd joined the Constitutional Democratic Party before Lenin sent him, along with other intellectuals, into exile in 1922 to Prague.

Here, he studied under S. N. Prokopovich; the eminent Russian economist who preached the benefits of central planning. Once in England, Baykov convinced British political leaders such as Clement Attlee and Harold Wilson of the pressing need to study the Soviet experience and apply it selectively to nationalized British industry in the immediate post-war years. He wasn't afraid to recruit staff who were known communists, like Davies and Barker (who later left the Party after Khrushchov's revelations of Stalinism at the 20th Party Congress in 1956). What an irony of history that I was able to reunite with Professor Baykov at the Higher Party School two years after my graduation, on his first return to Russia.

The third influential lecturer was an elderly Russian princess, Miss Koutaissov, who imparted her love of Russian literature to her students. She once told me, knowing how attracted I was to communism, that the two tragedies of Russian history constituted the Mongol–Tatar invasion in the early thirteenth century and the Bolshevik revolution in 1917. She lived to over a hundred but not to see the fall of her communism. Both Bob Davies and Geoff Barker communicated their respect and affection for Russia and its economic, military and social achievements, but also their objective analysis of the terrible political price the people paid in the purges and under Stalin's totalitarian system, opening my eyes to the sometimes brutal nature of the communist system, though not dimming my revolutionary ardour.

Outside of study, I attended a weekly Marxist discussion group for over a year at the home of the Professor of Classics, George Thompson. This was where I learned a great deal about Marx and his ideas. Professor Thompson and his wife were convinced communists and ran a socialist-oriented

Clarion choir besides Marxist classes. With a singing voice as sonorous as a croaking frog, I never aspired to be included in the choir.

My Russian Studies degree was to serve me well for my Soviet adventure. On the one hand, it prevented me from swallowing Stalinist propaganda, as some communists did, and on the other, from swallowing capitalist propaganda about Russia, as many Brits did.

I was three years older (it seemed a lifetime) than most of my fellow students, who had gone to university straight from school and had little experience of life. I celebrated my twenty-first birthday in October 1957, barely a week after arriving in Birmingham. I was lodging in a bedsit at the Harborne home of an elderly Black Country widow, Mrs Hilda Orton, with whom I corresponded right up to her death in the early 1970s, sending her Russian dolls and knick-knacks. In my search for digs I was surprised to see ads that stipulated 'No Blacks, No Dogs, No Irish', which excluded me with my Irish surname. Mrs Orton had no such prejudices.

Though still tongue-tied and lacking in debating skills, my examination results showed to my surprise that discipline, organization and sheer hard graft gave me the edge over younger students, eventually earning me an Upper Second Honours degree. No congratulations were forthcoming from my family, including the doubters. Not because they begrudged me academic success, but because my 2.1 Honours degree in Russian Studies meant as little to them as a Masonic handshake. My degree belonged to Them, not Us.

University life was also to provide further opportunities to promote my football career. We had well-organized inter-university tournaments and excellent pitches, gyms and training grounds. Moreover, Birmingham was the only

English university of the time to oblige *all* students to do at least two hours of sport per week throughout their first year. It was something Birmingham had in common with universities and colleges in Eastern Europe and the Soviet Union.

It was just my luck that National Service ended a couple of years after my demob. I had become pitchwise from playing alongside Cornishmen and Irish and Scots team-mates while in Germany. Perhaps that was why my game now had an added toughness that earned me the nickname 'Chopper' Riordan. My short-sightedness and lack of speed occasionally caused a late-ish tackle, chopping down a speedy opponent en route for goal.

For reasons I cannot now recall the nickname later followed me to Moscow where my team-mates invariably referred to me as *Topor*, ('Chopper'). I could count myself in good revolutionary company in that the Prime Minister Molotov still bore the alias *Molot* (meaning 'Hammer'), the old ('repressed') Bolshevik Kamenev was *Kamen* ('Rock'), and Stalin was the 'Man of Steel' (from *Stal*). Mind you, the writers Maxim Gorky and Demyan Bedny were respectively just 'Bitter' and 'Poor' – just like me.

While football hardened me, university life politicized and gentrified me – or, rather, turned a fairly ignorant, uncultured oaf into a questing and discriminating pseudo-intellectual. In the 1950s, Britain was still marked by its nostalgia for the diminishing Empire and deference to monarchy and the Christian Church. George Orwell aptly described the England of the fifties as 'the most class-ridden country under the sun. It is a land of snobbery and privilege, ruled largely by the old and silly.' That was certainly true of politics (the post-war Conservative governments of Churchill, Eden and Macmillan), the armed forces, the civil service, the Church and the BBC (run by the devout puritan Lord Reith).

But the worm was turning, as John Osborne was to show in his influential play *Look Back in Anger*, in which Jimmy Porter's plea for good, brave causes found a ready recruit in me. Twenty years before I would probably have volunteered for the International Brigade, fighting on the Republican side in the Spanish Civil War. A flavour of the era may be gained from northern working-class writers such as John Braine, Alan Sillitoe, Stan Barstow, Barry Hines and Keith Waterhouse. Young people were on the march against the values of the older generations and adult-imposed regulations, a trend that found its expression in clothing, hair styles and most prevalently pop music, especially that of the Beatles and the Rolling Stones in the UK and Elvis and Bill Haley in the USA.

In the spirit of the age, I'd been a Teddy Boy while in the school sixth form. I imagined I was the height of sartorial elegance in my knee-length jacket with its velvet collar, drainpipe rayon trousers, Slim Jim tie and winkle-picker or brothel-creeper suede shoes. At that stage, there was more swagger than substance in my clothing statement.

In the late fifties, there were plenty of causes to espouse: the Campaign for Nuclear Disarmament (CND) movement with its great annual marches from London's Trafalgar Square to Aldermaston in Berkshire, early opposition to the war in Vietnam, to Britain's attack on Egypt in 1956 (along with France and Israel) after President Nasser's nationalization of the Suez Canal, to apartheid in South Africa. From localized issues quite a few students and young people moved to universalistic politics and ideologies, joining left-wing parties and peace movements.

At the same time, other events occurred that made 1956 a defining year for many on the left. For communists the year was, in the words of communist historian Eric Hobsbawm, 'the political equivalent of a collective nervous breakdown'. In February, the Soviet Party leader Nikita Khrushchov had made his 'secret' speech at the 20th Congress of the Party which stunned communists the world over by exposing and condemning Stalin's crimes. Although some hard-liners in the British Party, like Rajani Palme Dutt (a loyal Stalinist), dismissed Stalin's 'mistakes' as mere 'spots on the sun', many were ashamed to realize they had been defending the indefensible for years and that their ideological opponents had been right all along. If that were not enough, the straw that broke many comrades' backs was the Hungarian uprising which, by chance, coincided with the British–French–Israeli invasion of Egypt in the autumn of 1956.

Condemnation of the RAF bombing of Cairo was bound to ring hollow when Soviet T-54 tanks were mowing down rebellious Hungarian workers in Budapest. The *Daily Worker* sent one of its top correspondents, Peter Fryer, to Budapest to report on the 'CIA-inspired counter-revolution'. He was shocked by what he found, and said so. But his dispatches were either ignored or heavily censored. Later, he wrote: 'The events in Hungary, far from being a fascist plot, were a revolution by the vast majority of the people against the despotic rule of the Stalinist bureaucracy.'

The cumulative effect of the 20th Party Congress and Hungary meant that, by January 1957, the British Communist Party, which clung to the Soviet line, had lost as many as 9,000 members, including leaders of the Fire Brigades Union and the Scottish miners – a quarter of its membership.

Despite the Hungarian uprising and Khrushchov's secret speech, which both occurred when I was as yet barely politically conscious, I joined the Communist Party of Great Britain in 1959, while still at university.

I was a socialist for moral and social background reasons. The Labour Party seemed to be espousing the wrong causes and clinging to Washington's coat-tails; to my mind its leaders were betraying the very class they claimed to represent. Labour Party socialism was not red-blooded enough for me. It eschewed revolution in favour of evolution and support for the exploiting class.

No one in my family or, indeed, no one I'd ever known personally when growing up, had been a communist. In fact, I can only recall coming into contact with one communist. An oddbod, Billy Russell, had stood on a soapbox on Southsea seafront on a Sunday afternoon, braving catcalls and a tiny hostile crowd. He was usually drowned out by hecklers and the neighbouring Salvation Army. We thought him as much a crackpot as the adjacent 'End is Nigh' billboard carriers. Indeed, poor old Billy did eventually crack up, ending his life in a mental home.

Though we were separated by a wide gulf of social privilege (not to mention him being a Southampton and me a Portsmouth supporter!), I agree with Ivor Montagu, born into the aristocracy and yet a lifelong communist and one-time deputy editor of the *Daily Worker*:

> What repelled me about society as it existed was its
> unfairness, the hypocrisy or complacency of its supporters,
> who either denied its ills or accepted them as irremediable,
> and saw nothing incongruous in their ready acceptance of
> its inherent advantages for themselves. What attracted me to

socialism was its reasonableness and morality, its insistence
on the feasibility of just realisation for all of inalienably
equal rights and opportunities.

Montagu was an extraordinary man. Son of Lord Swaythling,
a Jewish peer of the realm, he was founding president of the
English Table Tennis Federation at 18, and of the International Table Tennis Federation at 22, a post he held for
41 years, a record in any sporting body. He followed the usual
aristocratic path to Westminster public school and King's
College, Cambridge but then took the 'heretical' step of
joining the British Communist Party and becoming deputy
editor of the *Daily Worker*.

I only bumped into Comrade Ivor twice but both occasions
stick in the mind thanks to his warm and certainly idiosyn-
cratic charisma. The first time he recounted how he had
hectored Stalin just after the war about the need for the Soviet
Union to join the Olympic movement, a suggestion the
Politburo acceded to in 1951. And then many years later, on a
Saturday afternoon in 1981, I saw him at the annual general
meeting of the Society for Cultural Relations with the USSR
(he was president, I was a vice-president). In the break I went
up to him and, because he was wearing a hearing aid, shouted
in his ear. 'Not so loud, lad,' he said. 'I'm trying to listen to the
England v. Scotland football match.' Now there was a man with
the right priorities! I came to learn from him that the only
fanatics worth trusting are of the football variety.

Prior to my application for a Party card, I had been invited
as a new member of the fairly small British-Soviet Friendship
Society to be their student representative on a five-person
'delegation' to the Soviet Union. The BSFS was a pro-Soviet
organization that sought to improve relations between Britain

and the USSR. Only later did I discover that it was one of several communist fronts. I went to the Soviet Union in 1959 and had a whale of a time, though I cringe to recall the ridiculous speeches I must have made to the thousands on Moscow Radio and the gathered throngs in Moscow, Leningrad and Sverdlovsk. Seduced by my own importance, I assumed a sort of spiritual homecoming inspired by the warm welcome we received as 'brave fighters for British-Soviet friendship'. My studies had steeled me against the low standard of living and relative poverty of Russia in 1958. But visits to foundries (much like the one in which my stepfather worked) in the steel city of Sverdlovsk (now Yekaterinburg in the Ural mountain range), war museums in Leningrad, and textile mills in Moscow reinforced solidarity with a people who had suffered so much and were working hard to improve their lives. But I was never a sycophant and constantly asked questions about Trotsky and Stalin, the purges and one-party state that obviously irritated my fellow delegates and the Soviet Young Communists who accompanied us. Not for the first time I realized that Soviet and foreign communists were often 'united' by mutual incomprehension, as if talking back to back, rather than face-to-face.

After graduating from Birmingham University I did what most students did who could not bring themselves to work in capitalist industry: I trained to become a teacher, entering the London Institute of Education. My teaching practice brought me into contact with children in deprived areas of London, like Brixton and Streatham, and strengthened my resolve to help the underprivileged. Moving from the provinces to the capital took me to the heart of the protest movements, several of which I contributed to: peace, anti-racism, Vietnam. The move to London also brought me into contact with the headquarters of the Communist Party on King Street in Covent Garden, an austere grey building protected by opaque, thick glass squares. The insides were as grey as the outsides and saturated by the siege mentality of the comrades who worked there – the last remnants of a communist enclave now encircled by the oncoming capitalist hordes, or so they would have liked to imagine. Apart from portraits of Marx, Engels and Lenin adorning the walls, you could imagine yourself inside the officers' quarters of a reform school. A strange, unique place.

As I was coming to the end of my one-year postgraduate course, I discussed my future options with Betty Reid, a full-time official concerned with international relations. Betty offered me a choice: either to train as a student leader in Prague, or to take an unspecified course in Moscow. In so far as I have always been a follower, not a leader of men (or women), I plumped for the 'cradle' of the socialist revolution and 'capital of world communism'. Moscow sounded exciting. In any case, I spoke Russian, not Czech.

5

GOING HOME

So it was on 29 August 1961 that I set off by bus from Portsmouth to Heathrow with my new wife Annick, a French communist. Annick and I had met less than a year before at a nightclub where I was playing the double bass in a dance band. A trainee nurse, she had more or less run away from her farming parents in Picardy in Northern France, and developed communist leanings. Despite several warning signs that we were 'incompatible', we married on 4 July, some weeks before departing for Moscow. I later rationalized my problem with women in typically class terms. While working-class girls were intellectually unstimulating, I shared little common culture with middle-class girls, most of whom looked down on a rough diamond like me. I had gone out with a Portsmouth girl, Jeanette, for over three years. She had waited for me to complete National Service, only for me to end our relationship because I wanted to be free to travel and explore. After the hurt I caused her she emigrated to Australia and I never saw her again. Annick, being foreign, was free of the tell-tale signs of class – the differences in her language, culture, dress and politics made it simpler for me not to conflate how I felt emotionally with what I believed politically.

We met at Heathrow, as arranged, three young men in their early twenties. Londoner Roy Bull had been in the Party for four years, deputy student president at Leeds University and a member of the Yorkshire Party committee. Self-assured and dedicated to the cause, he had done his National Service in the Signals in North Africa and been on Party delegations to the German Democratic Republic (twice), the Soviet Union and Austria. Steve was a proud and generous cockney, as thin as a wraith, bespectacled and rarely seen in the waking hours without a fag in his mouth. Luckily for him, the time he spent asleep far outweighed that spent awake. He had been a Party member for eighteen months and chairman of his London district Young Communist League. He had done a history degree at London's King's College, worked as a postman and shop assistant, and spent two weeks working in the GDR.

Mike was a tall, gangly, short-sighted fellow with a strong Nottingham accent, five years our senior in Party membership. His pebble glasses gave him a sinister resemblance to the notorious police chief Beria. Of course, we never mentioned it to him – we weren't stupid! He'd gained a degree in Russian from Manchester University, during which time he had been chairman of the Federation of Socialist Students, Chair of Nottingham YCL, Chairman of his University Communist Party, a two-time delegate to the USSR, and British Party representative at the Finnish Party's 8th Youth Festival. Even more than Roy, Mike took our time in Moscow very seriously, measuring it in terms of its contribution to fostering communism in the UK.

None of us had the faintest idea about our ultimate destination. It was all on the QT, conspiratorial, nerve-tingling.

The secretive nature of our jaunt was heightened on the arrival of our Aeroflot Tu-104 at Moscow's Sheremetyevo Airport, where we were separated from the thronging crowd and ushered into an empty VIP lounge by a man who appeared to speak no English (in fact, he barely spoke at all). Waving us through customs without a check, he led the way to a black shiny limousine with curtained windows.

We were more bemused than intimidated or surprised. So this was it. Moscow. The Soviet Union. Our secular Mecca. We were quite pleased to be treated as VIPs, to be smuggled in, out of sight of watching British spies. From undesirable British nobodies, we were transformed into distinguished Soviet somebodies. Now I knew how British communist leaders must have felt on entering the 'promised land': one moment vilified in their own country, the next treated as revolutionary premiers-in-waiting for whom red carpets and limousines were their due. Three cheers for the revolution.

Our journey from the airport took about forty minutes. Through chinks in the limousine's black curtains, we glimpsed wooden huts, some horses and carts, rattling trams, headscarved old women in black, a broad river, some big anti-tank crosses that marked the closest the Nazis had come to Moscow (God, they had got *this* far?), dusty wide streets, long shops with identical names: *GASTRONOM*, *SPORT*, *APTEKA*, *RESTORAN*. It was a huge culture shock for us naïve Brits. Where were the football pitches and grounds that you passed in London? The cafés and pubs? The advertising hoardings? Here, the walls were festooned with posters of heroic men and women bearing workers' tools and wearing goggles to shield their eyes from blast furnaces. No happy, smiling faces; rather, down-turned and distracted as people hurried along with string bags and canvas carriers. Now and then there was a legless man on a wooden trolley, propelling himself with arm stumps. And – could it be? Yes, a few drunks, staggering from pillar to post.

Finally, our limo turned into a spacious square and pulled up before a large sandy-coloured building of solid Russian architecture. It reminded me of the Victorian buildings that remained standing in my home city after the German bombers had done their worst. This grand edifice was set back about two or three hundred metres from Moscow's main thoroughfare, Gorky Street (or, as it is called today by its pre-revolutionary name, Tverskaya Street), at its far end, near Belorussian Station. In front of it were pleasant gardens where I was shortly to be pushing my daughter Tania's pram and fending off verbal attacks by Moscow *babushki*, those same old grannies in headscarves we'd seen on the drive in, for not swaddling the baby.

We were escorted through the imposing entrance façade where we relinquished our passports, into an interior of further buildings – evidently lecture halls, canteens, shops, hostels and other accoutrements of a busy college, which this obviously was. Groups of students passed by without a glance at us, and the occasional black or brown face told us this was an international institution. Our taciturn guide did not enlighten us as to the place's name or designation. Instead, without a word, he stopped outside Block No. 8 and led us up to our accommodation on the fifth floor. Annick and I had a double room, No. 60, Steve got a room to himself next door to us, and Roy and Mike shared No. 48, next to an East German comrade on one side, and a couple on the other: the man was from Iran, the woman, Carmen, from Venezuela (they split up at the end of the course to bring revolution to their respective countries). The rooms smelled oddly of flea and cockroach powder. Each was equipped with washbasin, bed, desk, settee, wardrobe and telephone and, most peculiarly given Khrushchov's new anti-Stalin line, a portrait of Stalin on the wall. Down the corridor were a communal kitchen, showers and toilets.

Judging from the talk around us, our new neighbours were mostly Germans from the GDR. They turned out to be the largest group of foreigners in the place. After dumping our bags, we were taken to the canteen and treated to a grand meal of salami, sturgeon and tomatoes followed by steak and chips, fried eggs and cucumber washed down with lemonade; for dessert there was a bruised apple. His duties fulfilled, our silent guide slipped away and we were left to our own devices. My first thought was to write home and let Mum know where I was. She needed my address for the weekly pink football paper, so that I could keep up with Portsmouth's slide down the four divisions (since the paper arrived a fortnight late, Pompey had slid even further by the time I received it). Where were we? The question kept playing on our minds. Wandering about the spacious campus, we finally ended up outside on the square where we read the sign on the wall:

VYSSHAYA PARTIYNAYA SHKOLA
6 MIUSSKAYA PLOSHCHAD

'What does that mean?' Steve, the one-time postman wanted to know.

All of us had at least a smattering of Russian (important for when the revolution came in Britain!). Mike and I, indeed, had Russian degrees.

'Party School' was clear enough, but 'Higher' eluded Steve and Annick. It took time to sink in: this was as high as you could go!

THE HIGHER PARTY SCHOOL
6 MIUSSKAYA SQUARE

'Er, I think it means "Higher Party School. 6 Miusskaya Square".'

Fair enough. So that was what we wrote home to relatives.

I later learned that the grand building at which we had arrived had been built in 1907 as Moscow Public University, named after the liberal educationalist A. L. Shanyavsky. After the 1917 Revolution, it initially became a *likbez* (liquidate illiteracy) training college for illiterate Party activists before being handed over to the Communist International, the Comintern, in 1926 as a training base for foreign communists. This was the famous International Lenin School which, with the demise of the Comintern, became the Higher Party School for both Soviet and foreign comrades.

So much for keeping our Moscow mission quiet from MI5's prying eyes. Not that any of us much cared or saw the need for all the cloak and dagger stuff. It was only later that we realized the importance of security, especially for clandestine communists from such countries as Iran, still in those days ruled by the Shah. Some months afterwards, the lesson was hammered home when we learned that five young Portuguese comrades had been arrested and executed on returning home to Antonio Salazar's fascist regime. On one occasion, I was charged with breaking the news to the wife and two daughters of the Iraqi communist leader, Kassim, that he had been executed, an incredibly salutary experience (our two families were neighbours and my daughter used to play with their daughters). Pictures of those who sacrificed their lives for the revolution sometimes appeared on the School's entrance hall wall with a lighted candle beneath them.

So this was the Higher Party School, which none of us had ever heard of. Certainly, the Communist Party back in London had not mentioned the name, but they surely must have known of it. Its principal function was to ensure that future Soviet Party functionaries – Party secretaries, newspaper editors, diplomats – were given a good enough grounding in Marxism-Leninism to be able to argue the toss with doubters in whatever part of the country the Party chose to send them. But it was more than that. It continued the tradition of the pre-war Comintern International Lenin School, offering free political education to foreign communists, particularly workers who'd missed out on college.

The School's purpose, we were told, was given legitimacy by Lenin himself. His words to the 4th Congress of the Communist International in November 1922 were emblazoned above his white marble bust in the School's entrance hall:

> We must say both to Russians and to foreigners that the
> most important thing now is to learn . . . really to
> understand the organization, structure, methods and nature
> of revolutionary work. If this is done, I am certain that the
> prospects for worldwide revolution will be excellent.

Stalin had blessed those passing through the School's portals as 'people of a special mould', in other words professional revolutionaries.

Critics of the School might claim that its intention was to make sure that foreign communists were brainwashed with the Soviet version of historical events and current political strategy and tactics. Be that as it may – and my view would be rather more charitable – the HPS provided political education for communists from central and Eastern Europe (with the exception of Yugoslavia and Albania which had broken with the USSR over Soviet hegemony of the communist movement), for comrades from communist states in Asia (China, Mongolia, Vietnam, Laos, Cambodia, North Korea, Indonesia and India), for members of communist and worker parties in Africa, Asia and Latin America and, finally, for communists from capitalist states (Australia, Britain, Canada, Finland, Sweden, Italy, Spain and Portugal). The only major countries without representation during my time at the School were the USA and France. Some communist parties, like the Finnish, regularly took up their quota from the mid-1950s to the mid-1980s. Perhaps, being neighbours with the Soviet Union, they did not wish to antagonize the Soviet Party, or there may have been a more prosaic reason. As one of my Finnish friends and comrades attested: 'In Finland we never studied or ate properly – Moscow was the opposite.'

The entire costs of our tuition and accommodation were borne by our Soviet hosts, including our monthly grant of 180 roubles, nearly four times more than that given to top Soviet students. As far as I recall, we never openly questioned this disparity; it is an indication of our isolation from reality that we were not even aware of it for several months. When it was pointed out to us later by disgruntled Soviet colleagues, we made lame excuses about not having Soviet relatives to help supplement our income. But we all knew we were conniving in the widespread communist privileges and perquisites that existed. No excuses.

A couple of days after our arrival we were summoned to the Rector's office. Before entering we were asked to fill in a form, giving our personal details. Nothing too strenuous, but it did include one odd question: 'Social origin?' On reflection we all wrote the same: 'Working class', which was evidently what was wanted. It so happened that we were all, indeed, born into the working class, apart from Annick who was of farming stock. After a bit of chit-chat, the officious, bored-looking Rector squinted over his glasses and asked a question that took us aback:

'What aliases will you take?'

He sat, pen poised over our forms.

Aliases? We shook our heads. Perhaps he didn't know Britain. Maybe he didn't realize there was no persecution of communists and we had no need to hide our politics. The question appealed to my quirky sense of humour and I almost blurted out 'Trotsky' as my preferred *nom de révolution*. Despite the Rector's obvious incomprehension, we insisted on sticking to our birth names.

Straight from the Rector's office we were escorted to the school clinic where we underwent the most thorough medical examination we had ever had – by seven specialists, all women: a neurologist, dentist, optician, radiographer, phlebotomist, general physician and surgeon. Steve was informed he was twenty kilograms underweight and put on a diet of *kasha*: millet, oats, rice, buckwheat, pearl barley and some unidentifiable gruel. Oddly, the doctors didn't order him to stop smoking, even the foul-smelling Russian *papirosy* he'd been forced to buy for lack of Western brands.

Next we were whisked off to witness the lying-in-state in Trade Union House of Comrade William Z. Foster (1881–1961) of the Communist Party of the United States. He could hardly have had a grander send-off. Poor old Bill had come to Moscow in vain for a miracle cure for a heart condition. Dead, he received more honour and acclaim than he ever did alive.

A few days later we were taken on another macabre trip, this time to the Mausoleum on Red Square to pay our respects to Lenin and Stalin whose bodies were preserved in glass coffins there. I must confess to a sense of morbid curiosity rather than the mystical reverence that our hosts doubtless expected. Lenin resembled a dusty wax-like exhibit out of Madame Tussaud's, while Stalin, dead for the last eight years and raised significantly higher on his plinth than his predecessor, looked almost as good as new: his iron-grey hair was neatly brushed, the flowing moustache was clipped, the wolfish eyes were closed, and yet, like Dracula's, looked as if they could open at any moment! A month later, however, after an old Bolshevik, D. A. Lazurkina, told delegates at the 21st Party Congress (1961)that she'd had a dream in which Lenin complained to her about having Stalin as bedfellow, Stalin's corpse was removed and buried under a simple column and bust beside the Kremlin Wall. So we must have been among the last eyewitnesses to see Uncle Joe's body. Shortly after the Mausoleum visit, our cleaning maid, Valentina, took down Stalin's portrait from our rooms.

That was not quite the end of the story. Having a stomach upset one day, I booked into the School clinic. Also in the waiting room was another student, sitting beneath a picture of Lenin convalescing at Gorki, near Moscow. Involuntarily, I exclaimed in Russian, 'Good grief! I could have sworn that last week Stalin was sitting on the other side of the table!'

My fellow student stood up to stare at the print. Sure enough, someone had erased Stalin from the picture; the paint was barely dry. 'That's what happens to fallen heroes,' muttered my colleague.

His words could not have been more prophetic. That student turned out to be Alexander Dubček who, six and a half years later, as leader of his country, was briefly to lead the 'velvet revolution' in Czechoslovakia before being removed by invading Soviet forces and sent to work in the Bohemian forests. *That's what happens to fallen heroes . . .*

Ours was the first (and last) post-war band of communists sent by the British Communist Party to Moscow. No doubt the offer was there, but it was not taken up again. I later asked Betty Reid why the scheme hadn't continued and she made several suggestions. One reason was the much-criticized (by Soviet officials) lack of appreciation of theoretical grounding by British communists. British Party officials had never seen the need for their young people to study courses on Marxist Philosophy, Political Economy, History of the Working Class Movement and, especially, the History of the Communist Party of the Soviet Union – at least not in the way they were taught in Moscow. The British Party leader Harry Pollitt once criticized the pre-war School for turning out comrades who spoke in Moscow jargon: 'I have noticed many comrades who in England could talk simply and clearly to the workers . . . [yet they] get back [from Moscow] speaking a foreign language.'

The then Party Secretary, John Gollan, later told Steve that he had been firmly against our going to Moscow altogether. When the Nottingham comrade asked to be brought back early, Gollan's handwritten comment on the letter (which I later read in the Manchester Communist Party Archive) is telling: 'We should bring the whole lot back! It confirms my idea that we have been swindled.' Perhaps he shared the view of the French Party leader, Maurice Thorez, that, following the 20th Soviet Party Congress, 'we should treat with caution the History of the Communist Party of the Soviet Union . . . For the French Communist Party, the essential thing is the history of the French labour movement; it is around this history that we should organize our studies.' It would appear that few, if any, French communists attended the HPS after that. What exactly Johnnie Gollan meant by 'we have been swindled' I never discovered.

It would be wrong to think that all our classes were propagandizing or uninteresting; most were well prepared and illuminating. We were lucky to have an excellent Russian teacher, Vitaly Kostomarov, later to become Academician and head of the Mapryal Russian Language Organization. In addition, we had regular 'guest' lectures, in the auditorium where Lenin once spoke, from world-famous personalities like the first man in space, Yuri Gagarin, the then Soviet President Leonid Brezhnev, and foreign communist leaders like Cuba's Blas Roca, Canada's Tim Buck, India's Communist Party leader Ghosh and Spain's Dolores Ibarurri ('La Pasionaria'), heroine of the Spanish Civil War.

Of the many privileges afforded to us foreign communists, undoubtedly one of the most exciting and inspiring was the invitations we received to meet and socialize with the guest lecturers. Yuri Gagarin remains longest in the memory. Dressed in his tight blue airforce uniform, he was an extremely modest, welcoming and friendly man. His open fresh-faced appearance was, however, marred by a deep scar over his left eye. Only later, after his untimely death as a test pilot, did we learn of his descent into drunkenness (which also accounted for the scar, picked up from falling from a window). We also suspected Brezhnev of being partial to the bottle, thanks mainly to his slurred speech and awkward mannerisms. In fact, when we met him, in the summer of 1962, he had just recovered from a mild stroke and only two years later would be sufficiently recovered to seize power from Khrushchov in October 1964.

Another reason for the British CP to boycott the Higher Party School, suggested Betty, was that some British leaders remembered the fate that befell British communists in Moscow under Stalin, including those who had studied at the International Lenin School, the School's previous incarnation. Sadly, I knew nothing of this, nor did my comrades. Had we known, we might never have gone near the place.

As subsequent events were to demonstrate, there might have been a more mundane reason for the reluctance to send British communists to Moscow or for the Soviet authorities to accept them: the phlegmatic attitude of us British. The members of our party were certainly not very compliant or obedient; Steve was a gregarious character who would often sit around drinking and chatting into the wee small hours and so would regularly get up too late for morning lectures. Annick, being pregnant, left the course early. That left four. Mike, homesick and alienated by Soviet life, became probably the first and last student in the School's history to pack it in and go home, a year into the eighteen-month course (sixteen months' study plus two months' travel and practical experience on factory and farm visits). In his letter to Betty Reid, he wrote:

> We all agree on the absolute value of studying Marxism-Leninism and getting to know something about Soviet life at first-hand, but I have certain reservations about the course which are not fully shared by the others . . . What

worries me most about this type of course is the long time
(16 months) devoted to study – a period in which there can
be no linking of theory and practice, due to the
circumstances in which we find ourselves . . . I also
feel that to some extent we are divorced from life
at the Higher Party School.

The Party hierarchy was 'fully in agreement with [the] request', as the Manchester archive attests. With our comrade gone, only three of us were left attending classes. Then my two other comrades 'disgraced themselves' by refusing to attend any more Soviet Party History lectures. The subject was baffling enough at the best of times: so many goodies becoming baddies, 'repressed' old Bolsheviks turning out to be anti-Soviet agents and foreign spies; Trotsky, it was 'discovered', had been in the pay of at least *three* foreign powers. But when Comrade Nikolai Granin told us that the infamous police chief Beria had been executed in 1953 after vigilant Soviet leaders had found that he had been working for British imperialism, something snapped. Though communists, we resented having Beria linked with *our* imperialists. We knew it was utter tosh.

It was time to call in the red cavalry. We were summoned to a meeting with the *Daily Worker* Moscow correspondent, Dennis Ogden. Now, Dennis was a decent, honest Cheshire man, the best post-war Moscow correspondent the Party ever had. He had got into hot water with the authorities himself for refusing to reveal the sources for his cosmonaut stories (Dennis had been the originator of the story that Vladimir Ilyushin, son of the famous Soviet aircraft designer, rather than Yuri Gagarin, had been the first man into orbit). Dennis did his best politely to explain to us that complaints had reached the ears of the Soviet Party Central Committee and that we were compromising fraternal relations. Could we somehow try to play the game according to the rules? It might not be cricket, but we should try to play a straight bat.

We promised to do our best – Scout's honour – but it wasn't easy. That is not to say that we disliked lessons; there was much we enjoyed. One lesson we Brits regularly attended was choir practice, even if the choice of songs was somewhat limited. One of the 'favourites' was *Partiya nash rulevoi* – 'The Party Is Our Rudder':

> *The Party has united all our peoples*
> *In a single workers' state.*
> *The Party is our hope and strength,*
> *The Party is our rudder!*
>
> *Under the sun of the homeland, we are becoming*
> *stronger every year,*
>
> *We steadfastly hold true to Lenin's cause.*
> *The Communist Party of the country*
> *Calls on the Soviet people to do heroic deeds!*

In march time . . . Shame about the words.

When our attempts to improve punctuality and attendance proved unavailing, we next had a visit from James Klugmann, in late 1961, who had travelled all the way from London. We were driven in a big black limousine to the Party hotel off the Arbat (today one of Moscow's more touristy streets) and taken to a spacious apartment where we were met by Alexander Molchanov, head of the Central Committee Department for Relations with Foreign Communist Parties. He introduced us to Klugmann.

Now, Comrade Klugmann was someone we respected. Editor of the theoretical monthly *Marxism Today*, he had gained a first-class honours degree in French and German at Cambridge and was one of the British Party's leading intellectuals. He looked and sounded the part: bald, stocky, bespectacled, with a posh accent, he was clearly not your average Party official (top Party brass, like the Secretary, had to have a solid working-class background). This was the man who had nurtured the Cambridge spy network of Philby, Burgess, Maclean and, as it would turn out, Blunt. No doubt he would meet his old friends Burgess and Maclean (with whom he had attended Gresham's public school as a boy) while in Moscow. Once Molchanov had departed (in our limousine), Klugmann confessed that he sympathized with us and understood our objections to a Stalinist interpretation of history. But . . . for the sake of our Party would we try just a bit harder?

We said we would do our best.

A rueful personal conclusion I have to draw is that, in their radically different ways, both National Service and the Higher Party School failed miserably in their attempts to mould me into someone who'd be happy going with the grain. I made an unreliable soldier of the Crown and, even more so, of the revolution.

It wasn't only me. We were all upbraided by the School authorities and the Central Committee representatives for our candid defiance of the Soviet interpretation of history (like Beria being a British spy). I am certain that not for a minute did they doubt that they were in the right; as they would have seen it, they were simply following the Party line. The fact is that none of them had much, if any, experience of conditions abroad or of foreign communists. We 'infamous five' were even, albeit reluctantly, rapped over the knuckles by our own Party envoys.

The political pressure and discipline imposed by the Comintern in the 1920s and 1930s, before revelations of the purges and terror became generally known, might have worked with youthful British enthusiasts then, when fascism was on the upsurge in Europe. Now, the Comintern was defunct, Stalin's crimes had been exposed, our own Party leadership was lukewarm at best about the Soviet political education we were receiving. Within Russia we could see first-hand the negative as well as the positive facets of Soviet communism, even though, as Mike had written, we were 'divorced from life at the Higher Party School'. Perhaps there's something about the insular British that makes them less open to international cabals and all-embracing theories. We British communists were no exception.

6

MOSCOЩ REALITIES

For some people Soviet communism, with its allegiance to central planning over the free market, served as the perfect economic and social model for backward countries seeking rapid industrialization and full literacy. The Soviet Union had achieved swift, if uneven, industrialization and overtaken Western powers in no more than thirty years in the output of iron, steel, gas and coal; it had defeated Europe's strongest fascist military power, Nazi Germany; it was on a par militarily with the United States, including in nuclear capacity; Soviet state planning had obviated certain social evils characteristic of capitalism: at least officially, there were no unemployment, inflation, boom and bust economies. The country had a comprehensive system of free and universal education and health, it generously subsidized the performing arts and paid respect to high culture, avoiding the worst excesses of Western popular culture; and it was strongly committed to developing science and technology.

It had broadened access to sport, especially for women and ethnic minorities, and it had demonstrated through success at the Olympic Games, since its summer debut at Helsinki in

1952, that the socialist system was superior in many sports to that of its Western rivals. In 1957, it sent up the world's first artificial satellite, Sputnik, to circle the earth and, in 1960, followed with the first manned orbit of the globe, by Yuri Gagarin (and the first 'womanned' space flight, by Valentina Tereshkova, in 1963).

For the majority of its citizens, the Soviet government provided a peaceful, stable environment for them to live their lives and it came equipped with the vision of a bright future. Communist leaders seemed to know where they were going.

At home, Soviet people were generally proud that their armed forces and communist leadership had defeated the might of Germany and even acquired an empire stretching halfway round the continent of Eurasia. Even the Soviet domination of eastern and central Europe, the 'outer empire' – the establishment of one-party communist states formed by a mixture of force, intimidation and electoral fraud – was seen at home as the fruits of bitter war and a shield against future foreign attacks that had dogged their history and accounted for many millions of Russian lives.

What few people abroad, including us foreign communists, fully realized was how high the cost of victory in the war had been. It has taken until today for the Russian authorities to admit that twenty-four million Soviet civilians had died as a direct result of the Second World War. Furthermore, an estimated twenty million Red Army men and women, as well as partisans, also died in battle. That made a total of over forty-four million Soviet losses, by far the greatest number of fatalities suffered by a single nation during the war. The dead were not the only victims.

The Soviet Union of the early 1960s teemed with widows, orphans and invalids. The state could not cope with the physical rehabilitation of veterans left disabled at the end of military hostilities. That first glimpse I had had through the curtained windows of our car of a ragged, uniformed figure with no legs, pushing himself along with arm stumps on a home-made board was to be replicated time and time again, sometimes made less pleasant by the unfortunate's inebriated state. And who could blame him? Even sixteen years after the war, the point I arrived in Moscow, the scars were open and deep, and the wounds festered still.

One consequence of the war and the USSR's burgeoning status as a world power, which had repercussions for us foreign communists, was the hegemony of the Soviet Party over the world communist movement. What the Kremlin said was gospel for communists the world over. Even the Chinese Party under Mao Zedong, which had taken power in September 1949, acknowledged the CPSU as *primus inter pares*, first among equals. Like the 'people's democracies' of central and Eastern Europe, it had to follow the Soviet template for building a socialist state – however inappropriate that was for nations with different and sometimes superior economic and cultural development.

Relations with the CPSU were more filial than fraternal, and other worldwide communist parties had to follow and abruptly adapt to the line of the day. Any Party leader who demurred soon got the boot or was ostracized (as a 'social fascist' in Tito's case). An anecdote went the rounds about Todor Zhivkov, the ultra-loyal Bulgarian Party chief, who came to Moscow and sat down on a drawing pin. After jumping up with a howl, he removed the pin from the seat of his trousers, saw it was Russian, and immediately put it back, sitting down with an embarrassed smile.

It was not only the communist parties in power that had to do Soviet bidding. Stalin had imposed restraints on parties in the West, including the large and influential Italian, French and Greek communists who had played a major role in resistance to fascism in their own countries throughout the thirties. Right after the war, a number of communist leaders assumed that the Allied military victory would be followed by domestic political revolution. But, for example, the Italian leader Palmiro Togliatti and the French communist chief Maurice Thorez were instructed otherwise by Stalin and obeyed his orders. In Greece, the party ignored Stalin and tried to seize power. They paid the price as Uncle Joe stood aside while Britain and America helped the Greek monarchist forces to defeat the communist partisans.

Although revolution was not on the agenda in Britain, British CP leaders like Harry Pollitt and George Matthews had drafted a manifesto that talked of a peaceful, parliamentary road to socialism, a British way that avoided conflict. Whatever Stalin's feelings about this parting of the ways, he held a trump card that enforced obedience. Since the 1920s the British CP had been secretly receiving a direct subsidy from Moscow, in cash via the Soviet Embassy. This had stopped in the 1930s, but recommenced after 1957 and continued until 1979. Only a tiny handful of the British leadership knew about the money. It was one man's task, for a long period Party accountant Reuben Falber, to meet regularly and furtively with a Soviet Embassy official in a London park to pick up a bagful of money. Falber hid the money in his attic and, according to Francis Beckett in his 1998 history of the British Communist Party, *Enemy Within: The Rise and Fall of the British Communist Party*, dispensed it in sums that were not so large as to attract MI5 attention.

In addition, Moscow was helping to keep the Party newspaper afloat, the *Daily Worker*, renamed as the more socially appropriate *Morning Star* in 1966. In the mid-1960s, during my time in Moscow, the Soviet Union was buying as many as 12,000 copies a day, paid for a year in advance. That is one weighty reason why the journalists had to tread carefully in writing stories Moscow might not approve of, and further explains the British Party's concern for us to behave ourselves at the Party School.

Like virtually every other Party member, we students at the HPS knew nothing of this 'Moscow gold' and self-righteously refuted accusations that our Party was subsidized by Moscow. But it was this final exposure that added to the general disillusionment of many comrades later, after the 20th Soviet Party Congress in 1956. Of course, when you think about it, the free education we received in Moscow was a form of subsidy for British communism.

It bears pointing out that 'Moscow gold' pales into insignificance beside the wartime 'Lend-Lease' project and the post-war Marshall Plan which provided dollars and US goods and services that had to be paid for by the countries of Western Europe and which guaranteed political and economic subservience to the USA for many years after the war.

I had arrived in Moscow at an opportune moment. An ambitious Seven-Year Plan (all previous plans since 1928 had spanned five years) had come into effect in 1959, promising substantial, sometimes astronomical growth in industrial output, national income and even meat consumption. High-rise blocks of flats were rapidly replacing the quaint but bug-infested wooden huts in all cities; fridges, TVs and washing machines were entering popular ownership, and wages were on the up too, with virtually no direct tax paid. Rents, gas, electricity, telephone and transport remained inexpensive.

The Party Secretary Nikita Khrushchov, who had won his battle with the 'Stalinist faction', believed that a reformed Soviet order, with the Stalinist excesses removed, would quickly demonstrate its political and economic superiority over the West, and that capitalism would be seen as 'a dead herring in the moonlight, shining brightly as it rotted'. Not everyone shared his optimism. One joke of the time had Khrushchov lecturing an audience, boasting that 'we shall catch up and overtake America'. The first part of the statement gained applause, but an awkward silence descended at the second. Finally, an old man shuffled forward and muttered, 'Catch up, fine, but if we overtake, they'll see our backsides poking through our trousers!'

The helter-skelter advance had its problems. The quality of workmanship was poor, punctuality haphazard, commitment to work unreliable and drunkenness much in evidence, especially at football matches and in the countryside. Corruption was rife and defective reports to higher authorities were the norm. Accounts were fiddled, regulations on work practices and safety unobserved, and industrial progress was gained at great cost to the environment. This sometimes had tragic consequences. Robert Service, the respected British historian of Russia and biographer of Lenin and Stalin, writes that in Kazakhstan Khrushchov's 'neglect of the effects of nuclear testing led to the deaths of thousands of people'.

To his credit, Khrushchov had rehabilitated millions of people, albeit many posthumously, and since 1956 millions of gulag victims had been returning from the camps.

Despite Khrushchov's reforms, however, much remained unchanged politically; the extensive network of informers was retained; elections continued to be an undemocratic ritual – you could vote only for or against the communist-approved candidate. In many ways, the Soviet Union was still a police state that held its citizens suspect, especially the few allowed to travel abroad and come into contact with foreigners.

Another incomprehensible feature of society for us who had chosen our politics fully aware of the risk to our careers was the wide range of perks that political bigwigs – even 'smallwigs' – awarded themselves. I puzzled over posters which baldly announced that an opera or ballet performance was exclusively reserved for Party Central Committee members and their families (and no doubt hangers-on of every hue). I shook my head when I learned of the special shops, hospitals, canteens and rest homes only available to persons of political import.

As minor guests at the high table of privilege, we British students were invited to use the 'closed store' within the vast 'GUM' shopping arcade on Red Square. No one seemed to give a thought to what such a 'closed store' had to do with a society or Party dedicated to social egalitarianism. Few of these doubts fully surfaced until I had been living in Moscow for more than a few months or even years. From an early stage, the notion was steadily forming in my mind that a tacit agreement existed between the regime and society. It was not dissimilar to Juvenal's *panem et circenses* – bread and circuses – that dominated ancient Rome. You keep us safe and secure, divert us with world sporting performances and 'circuses' at home, and provide us with 'bread', a decent-ish level of clothing, housing, food (and also drink) – not perhaps as high as in the wealthiest capitalist states (of which we see little anyway), but better than in the past – and we shall leave the politics to you.

It is a contract that has proved difficult for subsequent, including non-communist, governments to tear up to this day, even if they had a will to do so.

I was quite prepared at this stage of my life to do my Party's bidding, thereby repaying them for sending me to Moscow. Betty Reid had indicated to me that I might take on full-time Party work in the Midlands on my return to Britain. It cannot have escaped her notice, however, that I had my doubts about many aspects of Soviet communism and my heavy conscience prevented me from toeing the line on the Soviet Union. I had written objecting to the Party newspaper's slavish following of Soviet policies (e.g. in regard to the stifling of literary criticism) in its correspondent's dispatches from Moscow. As a graduate in Soviet studies from Birmingham, London and Moscow, I was better equipped than most to pose intellectual arguments. Perhaps that is why the Party readily agreed to my request to stay on in Moscow.

7

A BODY TO BE PROTECTED

One oddity about the Party School, as we were to discover time and time again, was that its guardians apparently regarded our bodies as too precious to the revolutionary cause to allow us to play 'dangerous' games like football. Table tennis, volleyball, swimming were in – football, ice hockey and water polo were definitely out. In any case, there was no pitch or patch of earth in the vicinity for a kickaround. Pity. The school could have formed a formidable international team, combining the velvety skills of the Ivory Coast, Mali, Somalia, Senegal, Brazil, Spain and Portugal with the more robust talents of Germany, Australia, Italy and Great Britain.

For the African comrades, mostly from Francophone countries, the six months of snow and ice must have been a shock to the system, especially as the winter of 1961–2 was uncommonly cold, with temperatures tumbling to minus 30 degrees Celsius. Snow wasn't the only shock. Very few Russians had ever set eyes on black people before and their reactions to Africans walking down the street varied from intense stares to open racist hostility, especially if an African was accompanied by a Soviet woman. Not all Muscovites shared the declared communist dedication to internationalism and assistance to developing countries. While we Brits could pass for Russians (or Soviet Balts, if need be) wrapped up in our fur hats and coats, Africans were visible evidence of scarce funds being spent on foreigners.

Mine and Annick's closest friends were a middle-aged Canadian couple, Elsie and Bill Beeching. Bill had served in the International Brigade during the Spanish Civil War, and both he and Elsie were convinced of the coming communist revolution throughout the world. After all, once-enslaved nations in Africa and Asia were casting off their colonial shackles and opting for socialism, not capitalism: Mali, Senegal, Guinea, Angola, Ghana in Africa; and China, Vietnam, Laos and Cambodia in Asia. Even Cuba, on the American continent, had 'gone communist' under Fidel Castro. So things were looking rosy, if not quite red just yet.

Since my football career was at a standstill, I took to going to the Lenin Stadium to support the home team, Moscow Spartak. The club was very much the fans' favourite in the capital, rather like the Chelsea of the time in London. Like Chelsea, too, Spartak attracted intellectuals and artists, among them the writers Lev Kassil and Yuri Trifonov, the singer Leonid Utyosov and the composer Dmitri Shostakovich (who, curiously, was also a qualified referee). The style of play differed markedly from what I was used to at home: a slow, patient build-up, short, accurate passing, good first touch, versatile players who frequently interchanged positions – just as Moscow Dinamo had played during their immediate post-war tour of Great Britain, in fact. Violent play (such as charging the goalkeeper) was mostly absent, though obstruction, holding and pushing were much in evidence. Few defences hoofed the ball aimlessly downfield, and the entire team showed more tactical ingenuity and basic skills than generally on show in England.

In the 1961 season, one or two players stood out: Spartak's captain, and also the national captain, the famous Igor Netto at left-half (in his cultured play he reminded me of Portsmouth's elegant left-half, Jimmy Dickinson), and a speedy attacker with the un-Russian name of Valery Reingold (of Russian–German extraction). The following season the team was reinforced by full-back Gennady Logofet, whom I got to know well on and off the field, and a stocky dark-haired Tatar inside-forward, Galimzhan Khusainov, whom I was to meet up with forty-four years later when his hair had turned white. The team had ended the 1960 season in seventh place (out of sixteen), a disappointment after completing the double just two years previously in 1958; it came third in 1961.

Football in Russia has always been a summer game, the six-month season lasting from the traditional kick-off on May Day to early October. With the temperature invariably below freezing from November to April, ice hockey takes over as the No. 1 spectator sport. In my day, all stadiums were open to the elements, and in the 1960s the Lenin Stadium, a vast amphitheatre seating up to 100,000 people, would regularly attract between 60,000 and 80,000 spectators.

It did not take me long to realize that football played a special role in Soviet society. The stadium was somewhere you could let off steam, curse and shout abuse at authority (in the shape of the referee and linesmen). Perhaps that is why Russians call fans *bolelshchiki* – 'sufferers' or 'sick people'. This letting off steam has often been the case in countries where football grounds have offered provision for working-class, political or ethnic (as for Catalans in Francoist Spain) opposition to Establishment-imposed paraphernalia like national anthems, dress code or simply language and hymns that are 'not ours'. The British sports sociologist Eric Dunning has referred to spectator sports that have allowed people to carve out 'enclaves of autonomy', where 'mass audiences' can evade the 'goals of those who seek to control them'. Specifically in reference to Soviet football, the American historian Robert Edelman has remarked that fans found in football 'a way to demonstrate a measure of agency denied them in other parts of their lives'.

For Spartak, being independent of the state's paramilitary organs (Dinamo were the police team, TsSKA the army) and instead being sponsored by civilian organizations (white-collar trade unions), meant playing the the role of the 'people's club'. By no means anti-regime: more anti-Establishment. As one fan put it, supporting Spartak was for him a 'small way of saying no'; 'No' to all the suffocating rules and supervision; 'No' to the puritans who banned rosettes, scarves, flags, banners, rattles in the stadium; 'No' to the conservative 'Stalinists' (of Dinamo and TsSKA) who impeded the de-Stalinization process of liberalization. In so far as the all-seater Soviet stadiums were ringed by soldiers in the front row, and guarded by the military all the way from the metro station to the ground, the 'Nos' did not often extend to overt disobedience of unwritten political rules, like shouting obscenities at VIPs or hurling racist abuse at opposing teams (from Georgia or Armenia, for example), as sometimes occurred in regard to black footballers at British football grounds of the time. They were passionate, but they weren't stupid.

Interestingly, liberal democratic societies, such as Britain, made no effort to seduce fans with monumental constructions.

My paternal grandparents, Grandad from County Cork and Grandma from the Isle of Wight.

Happier days:
my parents' wedding, 1935.

In Portsmouth in early September 1939, just before war broke out. I was nearly three.

Gathering blackberries in Cornwall during evacuation in 1943.

My Mum's back garden in Portsmouth. My step-brother Terry is on the extreme right, next to my stepfather Ron. My step-sisters Marilyn and Jen are in the middle with Uncle George behind. Mum is at the back on the left.

A photo from my days at SGS (Southern Grammar School). I'm sitting down, second from right.

Corporal Jim (front right) with other RAF erks outside the billet in Bodmin.

In the Duke of Cornwall Light Infantry football team, 1955. I'm the beanpole sticking out in the middle.

Bluffing my way through as the double bass player in our university band.

Fraternising with
Soviet soldiers in
East Berlin, 1956.

The Teddy boy with Elvis quiff
up front and duck's ass at the
back, off-camera.

Playing for the British Army on the Rhine, 1955-56.

The mean machine: Portsmouth Dockyard League Division 8, 1955, just before call up to National Service.

ВЫПИСКА ИЗ ПРИКАЗА № 321

ПО ВЫСШЕЙ ПАРТИЙНОЙ ШКОЛЕ при ЦК КПСС

гор. Москва   5 сентября 1961 года

Зачислить слушателями полуторагодичных курсов
при ВПШ при ЦК КПСС следующих товарищей:

3. Риордан Джеймс с 29 августа с.г.

Ректор ВПШ при ЦК КПСС   (Митронов)
Верно:

ВЫПИСКА ИЗ ПРИКАЗА № 3/582

ПО ВЫСШЕЙ ПАРТИЙНОЙ ШКОЛЕ при ЦК КПСС

гор. Москва   30 декабря 1962 года

В связи с окончанием полуторагодичных курсов при
ВПШ при ЦК КПСС отчислить из состава слушателей курсов
следующих товарищей:

2. Риордан Джеймс   с 1 января 1963г.

Ректор ВПШ при ЦК КПСС   - Митронов
Верно:

The form I filled in on arrival at the HPS (Higher Party School), September 1961. It reads, 'Form by Order No. 321 for the Higher Party School attached to the Central Committee of the Communist Party of the Soviet Union. 18-month course.' Longwinded as ever!

Личный листок

по учёту кадров

1. Фамилия   РИОРДАН

имя ДЖЕЙМС ___ отчество ___

2. Пол М   3. Год, число и м-ц рождения 10·10·36

4. Место рождения АНГЛИЯ (ПОРТСМУТ)

5. Национальность АНГЛИЧАНИН/БРИТАНСКИЙ   6. Соц. происхождение РАБОЧИЙ КЛАСС

7. Партийность КПВБ   партстаж ОКТ 1958   партбилет № 1228

8. Состоите ли членом ВЛКСМ, с какого времени и № билета   НЕТ

9. Образование   ВЫСШЕЕ ОБРАЗОВАНИЕ

Название учебного заведения и его местонахождение	Факультет или отделение	Год поступления	Год окончания или ухода	Если не окончил, то с какого курса ушёл	Какую специальность получил в результате окончания учебного заведения, указать № диплома или удостоверения
БИРМИНГАМСКИЙ УНИВЕРСИТЕТ	ГУМ.ФАК-Т (РУССКИЕ НАУК)	1957	1960	—	B.SOC.SC (RUSSIAN STUDIES) СОЦ.НАУК (РУССКИЕ НАУКИ) 2:A
ЛОНДОНСКИЙ ИНСТИТУТ НАРОДНОГО ОБРАЗОВАНИЯ		ОКТ 1960	ИЮНЬ 1961		GENERAL CERTIFICATE OF УЧИТЕЛЬСКИЙ ДИПЛОМ EDUCATION

10. Какими иностранными языками и языками народов СССР владеете
РУССКИЙ, ФРАНЦУЗСКИЙ, НЕМЕЦКИЙ
свободно   свободно   читаю и могу объясняться

11. Ученая степень, ученое звание

12. Какие имеете научные труды и изобретения

The Moscow winter of 1961–2 had brass monkey temperatures of -30° centigrade. The *ushanka* (the typical Russian hat) came in mighty handy.

By contrast to the communist and fascist grand all-seater stadiums, my own 'palace of dreams' in Portsmouth, Fratton Park, was positively ramshackle, with most of the 20,000-plus crowd exposed to the elements while *standing* on the terraces. Despite its nineteenth-century design, I preferred its cosiness to the anonymity of the Lenin Stadium in Moscow.

It is tempting to compare the USSR and other totalitarian states, such as fascist Italy, Nazi Germany and Francoist Spain, in terms of the seditious use of football grounds as an opportunity for congregation and a forum at which to express dissidence. Certainly, all four totalitarian regimes tried, consciously or unconsciously, to outdo one another in building vast sports arenas. In the USSR, during the 1930s, the state set out to construct giant stadiums in the form of great amphitheatres set in pleasant natural surroundings – for example, the Bagirov Stadium in Baku on the Caspian Sea, which houses 80,000 spectators, the Kirov Stadium in Leningrad (St Petersburg), on the Gulf of Finland, with seating for 150,000, and the projected Stalin Izmailovsky Stadium in Moscow, for a staggering 350,000 spectators (the biggest in the world by a country mile), which, thankfully, was never completed.

Similar stadiums were built in a monumental style in the 1930s. In fascist Italy, for example, the regime constructed the 'Mussolini' Stadium in Turin for the World Student Games, the 'Littoriale' in Bologna, the Stadium 'della Vittoria' in Bari, the 'Berta' in Florence, the 'Edda Ciano Mussolini' in Livorno, the 'XXVIII Ottobre' in l'Aquila and, finally, the 'Citta dello Sport' in Rome.

Nazi Germany built the Berlin Olympic Stadium for the 1936 Olympic Games and, later, Falangist Spain constructed the Bernabeu Stadium for Franco's favourite club, Real

Madrid, naming it after Santiago Bernabeu, the Falangist president of the club from 1943 to his death in 1978.

This programme of grand stadium construction was not the sole similarity between totalitarian states with regard to sport. Sporting parades (with floats, banners, human pyramids and orderly exercises), marathons and gymnastic displays in the streets and squares were as common to the cities of the Soviet Union as they were to those of Italy and Germany in the latter part of the 1930s. Thousands of tanned, fit male and female bodies marched in close unison; they were extensively filmed and photographed for the benefit of both domestic and foreign audiences. In 1931, Soviet leaders announced an annual Physical Culture Day which was to become the apotheosis of Stalinist body culture. Such festivities were as much political theatre with sport as theme as they were a means of advertising Soviet sporting achievement.

Life in Moscow in the early 1960s was certainly not without its distractions. For me, there was always Friday evening at the British Consular Club, opposite the Ukraine Hotel on Kutuzovsky Prospect on the southern side of town. To get in all you had to do was flash your black and gold British passport – there was no need to declare whether you were for or against Her Majesty Queen Elizabeth II. Some of my comrades chided me for drinking with the class enemy, but British Embassy footmen (yes, *footmen*), minor servicemen, commercial salesmen and students were scarcely an imperialist coterie. It was from a footman, doubling as barman, that I heard of a Sunday morning kickabout for Diplomatic Corps personnel, on the Lenin Stadium reserve pitch.

'Come along, mate, with boots, plimsolls or bare feet,' he said.

No 'Who are you? One of us or not?' No wonder Burgess, Maclean and Philby found it so easy to spy within the Foreign Office for more than twenty years. But this was *football*: if you're a fan you're one of us. The 'bare feet' bit turned out to be no joke. When I turned up that Sunday morning with my football boots, I found a mixed diplomatic community under the command of the Kenyan Ambassador. He was shoeless but he did provide the ball and referee – his batman. It was all good fun, with Algerians, Kenyans, English and Scots, Brazilians, Argentinians and others all adding their spice to the football stew.

What with following Spartak and playing regular football with the Dipcorps, I had the idea of using my Moscow experience for writing a dissertation on Soviet sport. No one had ever told the story and it seemed an opportune time as people both in the East and West were waking up to Soviet sporting achievements. For historical information I needed to gain access to archives and hopefully a few sports buffs. The Party School could not help me, so I turned to *Dom druzhby*, Friendship House, a bizarre-looking seashell-encrusted mansion that had once belonged to the slightly deranged magnate Saava Morozov, who before the revolution had sponsored football among his mill workers, as well as contributing funds to revolutionary parties. Morozov's fairyland mansion was now the centre of 'friendship' with the Soviet Union, a sort of communist equivalent of the British Council, but with ampler funds and more explicit political guidance.

I had discovered that, through my British-Soviet Friendship Society contacts (I was now their Moscow correspondent), Friendship House could open doors for me that were shut to others. Sure enough, a meeting was arranged with a young footballer learning English; his ambition was to be a diplomat. Imagine my surprise when a tall, handsome young man appeared whom I recognized at once, even without his white shorts and red shirt: Gennady Logofet. I'd watched him play left back for both Spartak and the national team.

Gennady promised to show me round his sports college, the prestigious (and longwinded!) State Order of Lenin Institute of Physical Culture on Sirenevy Boulevard on the outskirts of Moscow. He explained that all full-time players, being nominally 'students', were supposed to combine their playing career with study for a future profession. Naturally, most chose coaching and PE teaching, though Gennady's hopes focused on work in foreign embassies (he is now a successful businessman).

It was my good fortune that the Soviet sports archives were housed at Gennady's Institute. In one of those many instances that undermined the impression of the Soviet Union as a secretive, impenetrable state, I became a regular visitor to the archives over the next four years without anyone ever demanding to see my documents or asking what I was doing. Thus it was, some fifteen years later (!), that I completed my dissertation and a book on Soviet sport. Thanks to Gennady, I discovered much about the origins of the game of football in Russia and the pioneering role of the British. We may not have invented the game, but we did provide unified rules and regulations which colonial administrators, missionaries, merchants, soldiers and sailors, and settlers took with them all over the world.

In the case of Russia, these British 'envoys' were primarily owners of local factories and mills, their managers and engineers, as well as members of the British Diplomatic Corps.

Their dominance over football in Russia lasted from the 1880s to about 1908, when Russian clubs were numerous and strong enough to beat – and usurp the positions of – their former instructors. Football was not the first sport for which the British formed a club. Back in 1860 they had set up the St Petersburg Cricket and Lawn Tennis Club (despite the weather).

In the early days the game was played first by the British among themselves and, a little later, by mixed teams of British and Russians, the latter being largely students, cadets and clerks in business houses. In 1894, Harry Charnock, general manager of the vast Morozov Mills (and one of four soccer-playing brothers from Blackburn who had come to Moscow in 1889 as consultants on cotton textiles), introduced the game to his workers. Harry had his workmen lay and mark out a pitch and raise goalposts; he ordered shirts, shorts and socks from England, all in the blue and white of his home team, Blackburn Rovers. Some say that the later adoption of blue by the first nationwide Soviet club, Dinamo (founded in 1923), was thanks to a warehouse full of Blackburn shirts being discovered. Boots proved too expensive, so Harry had studs fitted to the players' bast shoes (peasant shoes traditionally made from the bark of the silver birch tree). He said he relied on football to woo his employees away from vodka drinking on Sunday, the only work-free day of the week.

Harry's brother Willy had played centre-half for England and the brothers had all been members of Lancashire teams before departing for Russia. Another brother, Robert, gained notoriety later, after the 1917 Revolution, by being caught up in the so-called Reilly spy scandal (the infamous Sidney Reilly, born a Russian Jew and dubbed the 'Ace of Spies' for spying on

Russian defences for the British Embassy in Petrograd). He was not the only British sportsman to do time in Russia. The diplomat Robert Bruce Lockhart, who played for the Morozovtsy team in 1910, spent a year in gaol on spying charges. And the elder brother of Robert Baden-Powell was caught spying on Russian air balloon defences in St Petersburg while Robert was busy in Russia implanting Scouting and team games among the upper classes.

Although an outright ban on Russians joining the new football clubs was common in those days (the British did the same in India and France), the usual effective barrier was linguistic and financial. Activities, both sporting and social, were carried on in English, German or French (even today the *lingua franca* of international match officials all over the world is English). This was not a problem for the Russian aristocracy, to whom French was *de rigueur*, but it did present problems to the expanding Russian middle class who aspired to play fashionable foreign games. As in England, amateur football clubs also charged excessively high fees to keep artisans out of their private leisure garden. In any case, the Russian police kept a close eye on workers, who were not permitted to assemble in any uncontrolled group, such as in a game of football, at the turbulent turn of the century.

One cause for rising displeasure among the growing number of Russian footballers and fans was that Russian football administration was in the hands of foreigners – who were accused of often showing bias against Russian teams and players. For example, during 1903, official protests were lodged at the exclusion of all players of the Russian Sport team from the combined St Petersburg XI that played the league champions Victoria (an Anglo-German team) at the end of the season. Even worse, an English referee had sent off the

Russian player Chirtsov of Sport in a match against Nevsky (made up of British employees of the Neva Spinning Mill). Chirtsov was subsequently given a year's ban.

The Russians felt that Chirtsov had met with an injustice. As the newspaper *Sport* put it, he 'had been knocked to the snow and almost throttled by the English player Sharples in retaliation for a hard, but legitimate tackle'. Sharples, however, was exonerated by the (British) league officials. *Sport* continued:

> The League's decision is to disqualify Chirtsov for a year and to let off Sharples with a caution! This year we had Sharples the Throttler. Next year we could have Jim the Stabber (no relation) and Jack the Ripper! Match reports will read like crime reports. Will that gladden the hearts of Russian sportsmen? Certainly not. The British, in their typically high-handed way, having a large majority of votes, are banning a Russian who is totally innocent and letting off a man who is obviously dangerous, but one of their own. Let Russian clubs band together to form their own league. We are sure that a great future awaits football in Russia. But for that we can do with fewer Sharpleses!

The open admonishing of British officials and the call to Russian teams to form their own league were indications of the mounting popularity and strength of Russian football. The next year, 1904, for the first time saw as many Russian teams in the St Petersburg League as foreign teams. This increasing representation was further helped by the shock of 1905 when Russia was rocked by a wave of strikes and mounting violence (including the Bloody Sunday massacre of more than a thousand people outside the capital's Winter

Palace in January). A number of factory owners hastily began to set up sports clubs for their employees as a means of diverting energies from strikes and protests.

One aspect of the keen Russian–British rivalry was that it was drawing a relatively large number of spectators, especially when there was the prospect of a Russian victory. During the 1908 season, after the Russian team Sport had upset Victoria, an all-time record gate (for St Petersburg) of over 2,000 came to see the trial of strength when Sport met the British mill-workers' side Nevsky (which, to the crowd's delight the Russian team won).

In his memoirs, Robert Bruce Lockhart writes a mite optimistically that, had British entrepreneurs been able to spread the passion for playing football more quickly in Russia, the Whites might have won on the playing fields of Moscow what they lost in the Reading Room of the British Museum (where Karl Marx wrote philosophical works that were to influence and inspire socialists throughout the world). Lockhart regarded the introduction of football by the British in Russia as 'An immense step forward in the social life of the Russian workers and, if it had been adopted rapidly for all mills, *history might have been changed*' (my italics).

8

THE BЯITISH IИ MOSCOЩ

The Moscow Higher Party School had its origins immediately after the Russian Revolution. On 19 July 1920 the 2nd World Congress of the Communist International (commonly known as the Comintern) opened in Moscow with delegates coming from all over the world. The Comintern had come into being the year before to promote worldwide socialist revolution and to unite communist parties under a single leadership. Each national party was effectively to be a branch of the world party, with its permanent representative located in Moscow.

Britain was a country of particular interest to the Comintern in that it was the world's oldest capitalist state and, at the time, still its leading imperialist power; it had one of the best-developed labour movements, a large working class, and no peasantry. Fertile soil, one might have thought, for the seeds of revolution. At the time, however, Britain had a plethora of leftist groups and organizations, but no communist party. That was to be remedied soon after the Comintern Congress with the Communist Party of Great Britain being set up on 31 July 1920.

Another spin-off from the Comintern Congress was the setting up of a school for foreign communists in Moscow. The school's existence was never publicly admitted, and all its students had false papers. This was the forerunner of my own Higher Party School.

Initially, the International Lenin School (it took Lenin's name after he died in January 1924) provided free residential courses from six months to three years. In addition to its other students from all over the globe, it secretly trained an annual average of fifteen to sixteen mostly working-class British communists between 1926 and 1937, some 160 in all (like mill worker Maggie Jordan from Bradford and miner Allan Eaglesham from Dumfriesshire). Given the conspiratorial nature of the Lenin School, all students had to assume aliases, though, like us 'renegades' later, many did not take them very seriously: one called herself Mary Shelley (Frankenstein's creator), another Bernard Shaw. However, out of regard for the security concerns of other comrades and the Soviet mentors, they accepted their new names.

Graduates of the Lenin School included some people who were to become prominent figures in the British labour movement, like Welsh and Scottish miners' leaders Will Paynter and Alec Moffat, president of the National Union of Journalists Allen Hutt, *Daily Worker* editor Bill Rust and the International Brigade leader Peter Kerrigan. None of the graduates could aspire to the heights of people like Waldeck Rochet, head of the French Communist Party or Gus Hall of the US CP, or East Europe leaders after 1945: Tito of Yugoslavia, Gomulka of Poland, Honecker of East Germany and Alexander Dubček of Czechoslovakia (as mentioned earlier, at the Higher Party School at the same time as me).

Being tied so closely financially, politically and educationally to the Soviet Union ran other risks, as all communist parties discovered to their cost when Stalin launched a series of purges. The Great Terror that began in 1936 was to carry off British Party members who had settled in Moscow and taken Soviet citizenship.

To my great sadness, I never knew my fellow Lenin School students Rose Cohen or George Breslin, but I did get to know many other Moscow-based British people who suffered in the purges. I describe just three of them here. Tom Botting, a small, slim, dapper fellow, went to Moscow as a starry-eyed communist in the early 1930s. With his correct, accentless diction, he soon found work at Moscow Radio's English service where he rose to become one of the top newsreaders. It was when he was reading out dispatches from the Spanish Civil War in 1937 that he was suddenly confronted by the accusation of anti-Soviet slander. To his amazement, he was charged with announcing on air the previous day that 'Soviet ships had shelled Republican positions off the coast of Spain'. In response to his protestations that the tapes would show beyond doubt that he had said 'Hitlerite German', not 'Soviet', he was told that the tapes proved his guilt. He was never allowed to hear the tapes or to have them produced in court. Tom, like most of his British colleagues at Moscow Radio, was sent to a labour camp in freezing Kolyma in the north-west of Siberia for ten years. He survived, served his time and was let out in 1948, but was banned from Moscow. Eventually, after the 20th Party Congress in 1956, he was rehabilitated, permitted to return to Moscow and was re-employed at Moscow Radio (by the same people who had got him arrested).

Like almost all other political victims of Stalin's unreason, Tom *never* talked of his Siberian exile or his feelings towards the regime that had sent him there. Nor did I ever probe. In one candid moment, he did let slip that one of his erstwhile accusers had committed suicide, unable to face those he had falsely condemned. He said it very matter-of-factly, showing very little emotion. His experiences had taught him not to be loose with words.

Tom kindly got me a weekly slot on Moscow Radio, where I'd talk in English about my life and things I'd been up to that week. The programme was educational, aimed at language students rather than any hawkish watchers of England. I never discussed anything too revealing, although that didn't mean my pre-recorded talks were spared the censorship gauntlet:

'*I gave my girlfriend a box of chocolates for her birthday . . .* '

'Cut out "*of chocolates*"' – sugar had just been rationed in Moscow.

'*When I was growing up, my mother used to cut me thick slices of bread, doorsteps we called them . . .* '

'Cut out "*thick slices*" and "*doorsteps*"' – flour had also been rationed.

However petty this might seem now, I went along with it; Tom never saw the funny side. I can't blame him. As a recommitted Soviet citizen, he was never permitted to travel abroad and return to England. Humour was a commodity he could rarely afford.

George Hanna was square-jawed, with a bristling ginger moustache and could easily be mistaken for a sergeant-major in the British Army, which he once was. He and I met at my first job at Progress Publishers and worked together for three years. He had been attracted to the 'promised land' before the Second World War: 'It seemed a good idea at the time' he once told me. The Soviet Union was building a socialist society without capitalism and imperialism and George and many other comrades wanted to make their contribution. He married a fellow Londoner, Rose, and like me, had two daughters born in Moscow – Lucy and Anna. George and I often wondered who read the grotesque books and magazines we translated. After a while, we came to realize that it was best to focus on style, the mechanics of words, rather than content. Like other English translators – Bob Dalglish, Len Stoklitsky, Bernard Isaacs – we did our level best to produce readable texts, while ignoring their message.

In the xenophobic atmosphere that followed the victory in the Second World War (dubbed the 'Great Patriotic War' by Soviet historians), a new purge began against all foreign 'suspects', whether Jews, newly arrived Russians of White Guard parents in China, ex-Soviet POWs, or all foreigners living in the country. George was just one victim among thousands, if not hundreds of thousands (including refugees from Franco's Spain and Hitler's Germany). He was arrested almost immediately after the war on trumped-up espionage charges in which, it is rumoured, another British communist living in Moscow, Gabriel Cohen (falsely) testified against him. Cohen, who had worked for the Comintern, settled in Moscow where for the next thirty years he was known by his Lenin School alias, Tom Dexter. Dexter/Cohen escaped the purges and lived and died just round the corner from me in the so-called Red House – the home of many refugee Spanish Republicans. George Hanna on the other hand served eight years as a forced labourer in Norilsk in central Siberia. Meanwhile, on every book he had translated, his name was expunged with black ink. Imagine that: someone going through thousands of books to cross out George's name because he had become a non-person. During his interrogation, George had said in his defence that Harry Pollitt would vouch for him. Little did he know that the British communist leader was in the black book as a 'British Intelligence agent' too! George and his wife died in the 1970s. His two daughters, Anna and Lucy now live in Britain.

Len Wincott was a close friend with whom I spent many happy hours, including enjoying an entire summer sharing a dacha (in fact, the two front rooms of a collective farmer's house) in the picturesque village of Pushkin outside Moscow. He had been an able seaman for eight years when, in 1931, the government cut sailors' wages by a quarter. At the time Len was a crew member on a ship moored in Scotland's Cromarty Firth. He was one of the seamen who signed a round robin protesting at the cuts and threatening strike action – a 'mutiny' in naval terms. When the commanding officer invited sailors' leaders to come forward for negotiations, Len was nominated. The moment he reported for talks he was arrested and dishonourably discharged from the Navy.

Blacklisted by employers, he was taken under the wing of the Communist Party and spoke at their public meetings. As leader of the Invergordon Mutiny, as it became known, Len was seen as the hero of a courageous revolutionary action. In 1934, the Party sent him to Leningrad where work was found for him in the international seamen's club. The war caught him and his Russian wife in besieged Leningrad where he was employed to gather up corpses left on the streets and to transport them on wheelbarrows to burial grounds (Len said the corpses were often cannibalized by starving familes). For his work during the terrible Nazi siege he was awarded the Defence of Leningrad medal, of which he was very proud.

Three days after the end of the war, Len was arrested and sentenced to ten years' 'corrective labour' for 'anti-Soviet slander'. An elderly woman said that she had heard him telling a joke against Stalin. Like most old salts, Len was always full of jokes and did not deny that he could well have said something incautious in an off-guard moment. He spent his time working in an open-cast coal mine in the frozen wastes of Komi, beyond the Arctic Circle. As it turned out, he was not the only Englishman in the camp; he was joined by a British Nazi sympathizer arrested in Berlin after the war. Together the communist and the fascist put on music-hall items, including a 'black and white minstrel show', for inmates and guards alike. However, their entertainment was not to last long as the fascist was traded in a political swap, while Len the communist not only saw out his time, but lived in exile for an additional year, returning only in 1956. While he was in the camp, Len's Leningrad wife had died of cancer, and Len now married a fellow *terroristka* from a neighbouring camp, whom he met during his exile. They went to Moscow, rehabilitated under the Khrushchov amnesty, and Len embarked on a series of English-language jobs, dubbing movies for Mosfilm, teaching English, doing programmes for Moscow Radio and writing articles. When I met him, he was in his mid-fifties. Stocky, bald, with smiling eyes and a strong Leicester accent, he had an astonishing memory and could sing the words of most popular music-hall songs of the 1920s and 1930s, though never in tune.

As far as I know, no one in the British Communist Party leadership lifted a finger to help Len Wincott. A leading member, Andrew Rothstein, once told me that Len would return to England 'over my dead body'. Although the British CP was privately told in 1956 that Wincott had been released, they were instructed by Moscow to keep quiet about it – as with other Stalin purge victims. There were more than a few who believed that Stalin would not have arrested people like Len without cause. What both Soviet and British CP leaders feared most was that Len would return home and spill the beans about the 'red terror', or, as Len always said bitterly of communists, 'Red Quislings'. He had reason to be bitter.

Len did return to England, in 1974, through the help of the *Daily Express*. The Communist Party ignored him and he ignored it. Len himself said little of his experiences for fear of retaliation against his new young wife, awaiting his return in Moscow. The next time Len came back to England it was to have his ashes scattered over the Solent – within view of my window as I write this. He had always threatened his 'terrorist' wife, when she said how much she looked forward to dancing on his grave, that he was glad . . . because he wanted to be buried at sea. He had his wish.

Tom, George and Len were just three of probably scores, maybe hundreds, of one-time British communists, induced to surrender their British passports, who suffered in the purges. Theirs is a tragic story of faith betrayed. What is unforgivable is the lack of help or even concern of those British communists in London who knew of their fate and did nothing to save their lives or help set them free.

For me it was one thing blaming such gross miscarriages of justice on Stalin; it was quite another accepting British communist complicity in such crimes. Stalin had tortured and murdered innocent comrades like Rose Cohen and George Breslin, had interrogated and imprisoned Tom, George and Len, and many more. Yet CPGB leaders who knew about it had swept the whole business under the carpet. Why? For fear of their propaganda value to anti-communists? For fear of exposing the connivance of British communist leaders in lies and murders? For fear of offending Soviet sensibilities and disobeying Soviet commands?

I lived and worked with these wronged people. They were my close friends. The mistake they had made was to take Soviet citizenship as war clouds gathered in Europe. That put them beyond the power of the British Foreign Office. I venture to suggest that their 'class enemies' in the FO did more to help save them than their comrades in the CPGB ever did. As an example, in March 1938 the Foreign Office, through its Ambassador, Viscount Chilston, lodged a formal protest at Rose Cohen's arrest. In a letter to the Foreign Secretary, he wrote: 'We may be sure that . . . if we allow the arrest of one British subject, however undesirable, to pass unchallenged, it will be followed . . . by further arrests, next time probably involving persons more deserving of our protection.'

When the Soviet authorities replied that Rose had surrendered her British passport and was now a Soviet citizen, the Foreign Secretary, Lord Halifax, confessed that there was nothing he could do. She was shot soon after.

The British communist leaders who knew of the arrest made no public statement. When Freda Utley, the English widow of one victim of the purges, spoke out in London about communist silence, the CPGB General Secretary, Harry Pollitt, complained that 'She is absolutely foul in the way she is getting propaganda against the Soviet Union across.' So the unsullied image of the Soviet Union and Stalin was more important than saving innocent British victims of Stalinism.

I felt disgust and shame before my Moscow friends. It would have been too easy to leave the Party. Yet I took the tougher course of staying and fighting for the truth within the Party. I wrote letters from Moscow to Party headquarters in King Street, complaining of the false picture that successive *Daily Worker* Moscow correspondents were giving of Soviet life. I badgered Party visitors to Moscow. I wrote articles in communist publications, some of which were published. Eventually, my persistent campaign so annoyed Soviet Party officials that they planned to expel me.

I would beat them to it by buying my departure ticket.

9

PLAYING FOR
THE HOME SIDE

Halfway through the eighteen-month course at the Party School, on 12 April 1962, Annick gave birth to our first child, Tania, whom we called after a friendly Komsomol student at the School. As I was a new father studying at the prestigious HPS, the School administrators kindly made all the arrangements for my wife's (routine) ten-day stay at a Party Central Committee maternity home. For some strange reason, the draconian regime at the maternity home banned all visits and gifts. But round the back, with typical Russian ingenuity, knotted sheets had been rigged up to haul up various goodies, and proud mothers showed off their babies through the double windows. Since the babies were swaddled, on my first visit I could glimpse no more than a little pink face through the fifth-floor window. When Annick and Tania came home, we initially resisted a move from our single room in the HPS hostel. With my enthusiasm for the cause still buoyant, I believed that we communists could and should forego such privileges and luxuries as a flat to ourselves! No doubt such standing on (communist) principle was plain barmy to the hostel authorities, which included many Soviet Party members, who espoused a much more pragmatic viewpoint. Our resistance did not last long however. When Tania's night-time wailing constantly disturbed the beauty sleep of our hard-working East German neighbours, we surrendered and, a few months later, accepted the offer of a family flat on campus. Our next-door neighbours were the wife and two small daughters of the Iraqi communist leader Kassim (whose tragic fate was mentioned above).

Our succumbing to additional square metres – which was how Muscovites assessed their living space (How many square metres do you have?) – was not the only concession to bourgeois living. Following Mrs Kassim's lead, we took on a part-time maid to do the cleaning of flat and baby. That led to the occasional cultural misunderstanding. Despite our requests for Valentina Timofeyevna not to swaddle Tania, the nanny invariably trussed her up like one of Mum's suet puddings, with just enough space for Tania's button nose and magenta lips to poke through whenever she went out into the winter cold. Since Valentina persisted and knew more, as she would remind us, about the Russian winter than we did, we finally gave in.

What stuck in the gullet, however, was Valentina's shopping habits. She invariably brought home a far better cut of meat than I was able to procure. On enquiring how she did it, I was told she slipped the butcher at the Yeliseyevsky store on Gorky Street an extra 20–30 roubles above cost price. No, no, no, no, no! That was capitalist corruption! Undermining socialist morality! I wouldn't have it, even though she claimed that everyone did it. So we forewent prime joints and relied on meat dishes in the canteen (I never asked how they came by their food, even after I found a live cockroach in my cabbage salad).

Soon after Tania's birth, I received a letter from home curled up inside my pink football paper. It contained some startling news: Mum had decided to come to Moscow to see her first grandchild. Now, the furthest my mother had ever travelled was the forty-minute ferry trip across the Solent from Portsmouth to the Isle of Wight for her honeymoon. So to journey by train across Europe for forty-eight hours cooped up in a stuffy compartment with three strangers was a daring venture into the unknown. Remember too that this was the sixties when foreign travel was still the preserve of a privileged few and you'll have some idea of the extent of her undertaking. But Mum being Mum, she duly arrived at Belorussian Station towards the end of one June day in 1962. The only complaint she made was typical of her: she hadn't had a decent cup of tea since leaving home.

The Party School pulled out all the stops for her, a comrade's mother, no doubt mindful of the reverence for a communist's mother expressed in Gorky's novel *Mother*. When I asked permission for Mum to stay with us, the School staunchly refused. Instead, they presented her with an apartment to herself, free of charge, as well as food vouchers, a chauffeur-driven car, theatre tickets, and free visits to all the major museums – Museum of the Revolution, Lenin Museum, Lenin Mausoleum, Lenin's apartment in the Kremlin, etc. She graciously accepted all the hospitality and politely did the rounds of the museums and the Mausoleum. I wonder what she made of it all? The people around us speaking in an awed hush as lecturers pointed to the man hewn of stone, and bronze, and marble. Whether she thought we had all gone bonkers? Lenin's bald head and pointed little beard stalked us everywhere we went. Those intense, twinkling eyes peering out of canvas and squinting from plaster.

Mum bore it all in silent reverence, no doubt overwhelmed by the mystical treatment of the forty-year-dead Lenin. At the end of this exhausting homage to the first Soviet leader, she turned to our Party School guide and asked, in English, 'Who *is* this Lenin?'

Oh, Mum! How could you?

We had a good laugh about it later, especially at the guide's look of horror and incomprehension, and the utter silence that settled all around us, as people stared open-mouthed at this strange foreign woman who had never heard of their Lenin.

There was one aspect of Lenin that Mum spotted, yet we communists had failed to see: the complete lack of a sense of humour. None of the museums contained any evidence that he ever, throughout his life, had a light or humorous thought, a moment of fun, an evening of relaxed laughter. His eyes, however, as caught on newsreels and photographs, suggest differently; glinting with a spark of mischief and self-deprecation. But historically, like Jesus, the dead Lenin was not permitted to possess any frivolity. As translator of the three volumes of Lenin's Selected Works, I can vouch for that disregarded yet acute sense of humour, his love of comical satire in the Russian fabulist Saltykov-Shchedrin, and his quips about fellow socialists, as of Bernard Shaw: 'a good man fallen among Fabians'. Once he died, however, he ceased being funny. As George Orwell reminds us, 'Whatever is funny is subversive', especially when, like Snow White, you're a corpse in a glass coffin on public view.

I completed my eighteen months at the Higher Party School with an organized grand tour generously arranged for the Brits, Australians and Canadians. We visited Stalingrad,

Kiev and Odessa, then took a leisurely boat trip across the Black Sea to Batumi (the seashore still dominated by a giant statue of Stalin – he had lived there briefly in the early years of the twentieth century), then through Georgia, Armenia and Azerbaidzhan. Our English-speaking group could hardly complain that we had not seen life outside the capital or beyond the Russian heartlands.

Being with Aussies and Canadians certainly livened up our travelling group and prompted many a contest to anoint a Commonwealth Vodka Consumption Champion. Not that any of us could compete with the Georgians and their 'cha-cha', a devilish concoction made of grape pomace (the grape residual left after making wine), knocked back in one from tumblers. Blimey! Perhaps they imbibed it from birth alongside their mother's milk, which is how it managed to have no effect on them. Each time we went to drink it, their translator would propose a toast in English that kept us in stitches: 'Gentlemen, up your bottoms!' We took a team decision not to correct him.

Eagle eyes ensured that no Commonwealth back-sliders missed a turn or craftily watered a flower pot instead of gullet and belly. We did our best for Queen, Country and Revolution, but spent much of our 'fact-finding tour' in a fug of hazy inebriation. The weather did not help, it being late June with the mercury nudging 40 degrees Celsius.

On disembarking at Batumi, the one-time port of Colchis to which the Greek hero Jason came with his Argonauts to retrieve the Golden Fleece, we refreshed ourselves in our hotel rooms and ventured out on to the balcony for a view of Mount Kazbek on whose summit, in Greek myth, Prometheus had been chained for stealing fire from the gods and giving it to man. Trust an Aussie to spot other natural beauties. We lowered our gaze to the windows of a laundry opposite where naked Georgian women were sweltering in the steam. It was not a very comradely thing to do, ogle bare comrade ladies, especially in a place like Georgia where the men did not take kindly to others coveting their women. Next day, word of our misdeeds had spread and we were all upbraided by the Georgian Party Secretary. As punishment, we had to suffer even more rounds of cha-cha and toasts to mothers, sisters, wives, mistresses and slighted laundresses.

We were not sorry to escape from Batumi. Our coach journey took us through stunning countryside, along the old Military Road and up into the Georgian mountainside. It was rather like the English Lake District, only with warm sunshine, hills three times as steep and gushing alpine streams in which our guide cooled the beverages. Have you ever sat down to a meal with four bottles laid out for each guest: champagne, wine, vodka and brandy? And a warning that it was the height of rudeness to the hosts if just a drop is left in a single bottle?

Late in the day we rolled, almost literally, into the Georgian capital Tbilisi – named 'Tiflis' by a Russian tsar because he couldn't get his tongue round Tbilisi. My memory of our sojourn there is largely confined to eating and drinking. But as anyone who has visited the city will tell you, it plays host to a strange, human wonder: male singing. Like the Welsh, when men get together they sing in such harmony you wonder how they set to mind all the words and tunes. And once it gets going, the singing goes on for hours. I later shared an after-match drink with Tbilisi Dinamo Reserves, and their singing was as mellifluous as their ball skills – the Georgians being known as the 'Brazilians of the USSR'.

From Tbilisi we flew to Yerevan, the capital of neighbouring Armenia, in the shadow of the twin Ararat mountains across the border in Turkey, where the legendary Noah's Ark came to rest after the biblical Flood. For us Western comrades, more used to sips and slurps of amber and brown liquid, we now had to acquaint ourselves with a different flood: of dark brown Ararat brandy. Each toast ('To the bright communist future!' 'To the four great leaders!' Which four? Marx, Engels, Lenin and Stalin, or was there some Armenian in the pantheon we weren't aware of? 'To the Soviet family of nations!') came with a proud reminder that this cognac was Winston Churchill's favourite tipple. According to our hosts, it had helped him aid the Red Army in winning the war. So we owed our drink to the bulwark of Empire and Toryism!

One striking feature of Armenia was the obvious pride Armenians held in their culture and language. Streets and squares had names in Armenian script, and instead of tours of factories and housing estates, we were taken to churches and monasteries. Throughout the trip we were met by constant reminders of how much this ancient cultured people had suffered throughout their history: in the early twentieth century, for example, the Turks had tried to wipe them off the face of the earth, much as Hitler had tried with the Jews. Later, my footballing pals told me how Armenian fans were by far the most emotional and, at times, violent, of all Soviet supporters.

On to Baku, capital of Azerbaidzhan, situated above the Caspian Sea and pungently smelling of oil from the many derricks and refineries littered across its shoreline. Visits to tea and tobacco plantations were followed by hospitality at the hillside mansion of the Azerbaidzhan Party boss. After a bountiful dinner, we adjourned to the compound's cinema, but found the film of a Turkic opera too much for our bleary eyes and once again left a poor impression of ourselves. One thing that caught the eye in this republic was that, unlike the others we'd visited (Russia, Ukraine,

Georgia and Armenia), Azerbaidzhan was an Islamic state. That was evident in people's dress: men often wore turbans or their *tibeteka* base, while some women hid their faces behind the yashmak or even enveloped their bodies in the *parandzha*, the voluminous horse-hair veil that covered the body from top to toe. The Azeris were the Turkic-speaking kin of the Uzbeks and Turkmens at the other end of the Caspian. There was no thought then of Muslim extremism – the secret police saw to that.

The three sub-tropical Caucasian republics left an abiding impression on us of the Soviet Union as an inland empire, as opposed to the British overseas empire with its many far-strung and remote island colonies beyond oceans and mountains. Little did we know then that thirty years hence, this sprawling Soviet empire too was to go the way of the French and British and, similarly, was to revert to ethnic conflict and even medieval practices, including the exclusion of women from universities and positions of state in the Muslim countries (some on the border with Afghanistan).

Undoubtedly, the most memorable and awe-inspiring city on our round-Russia tour was Stalingrad. It was fewer than twenty years since the city had been pulverized, and the scars were still open and deep. Stalingrad marked the site of the turning point of World War II; this was the very first, and most telling, defeat of Hitler's armies. Throughout my time in the Soviet Union, wherever I went, people were eager to show how much they'd suffered in the war. There was no escaping it, and my pleas of war-site exhaustion or pacifism would go unheeded (no one was allowed to be a pacifist in Russia!). And so in Stalingrad: here is the house which Sergeant Pavlov held for over a month (no word that he later became a monk); here is the fifth floor ruined block of flats where the sniper Anatoly

Chekhov shot ten of his 242 German officers, where Tania Chernova 'broke 82 sticks' (her reference to the Germans she shot with her sniper's rifle); look at the River Volga swirling past the river port. How many thousands of bodies, Russian and German, found a watery grave there?

I cry easily. But I defy anyone to visit Stalingrad and remain dry-eyed. If our other visits were enjoyable tourist spots, Stalingrad was a stark reminder of what the Soviet people had suffered in the war, what feats of valour the Red Army and ordinary people had performed, and what a debt of gratitude the whole free world owes the Soviet Union. I'd been brought up in the naval dockyard city of Portsmouth which was hit badly in the Blitz (suffering almost a thousand deaths) and had still not fully recovered in the fifties. But Stalingrad was something else, the scene of hand-to-hand fighting, the graveyard of some three million people, more than were lost by Britain and the USA in the entire war. A huge stone monument of a Russian mother ('Mother Russia') wielding a sword dominated the city, standing atop the Mamayev Kurgan hill overlooking the Volga River. If anyone doubts what the war means to Russians, visit Stalingrad (since renamed Volgograd). I was to return forty-four years later, to present a programme for the BBC on the Russian war correspondent and author Vasily Grossman, who sent his dispatches from the doomed city. I was amazed and horrified to find they were still excavating bodies and war 'souvenirs'.

Our return to Moscow marked the completion of our course at the Higher Party School. We gained no certificate and attended no graduation ceremony inasmuch as the institution officially did not exist. On the whole, we remaining three British students agreed that we had enjoyed our time in

Moscow and greatly profited from it. Perhaps we would not go as far as interviewed Finnish comrades that 'it was the best time of their lives', but it was certainly a period that we never regretted and one that we would remember for the rest of our lives (and write books about!) – as much for the wonderful friendships we'd made with Soviet people as the hospitality and education given to us by the School. In terms of scholarly learning, however, our gains were less obvious, apart from the acquisition of Russian and our happy introduction to Russian literature. As any right-minded Russian would tell you, you cannot begin to understand the Russian soul without reading the literature. So I read it, old and new, good and bad, banned and tolerated. Russian writers had always been the conscience of the nation, the 'fourth estate' to quote a Russian saying. Now, in the atmosphere of a literary thaw (unfreezing books on once-forbidden subjects like the labour camps and Stalin's purges), encouraged by Party leader Khrushchov, like many people I was swept up in the excitement of the new literature, especially because I was being introduced to authors such as the children's poets Kornei Chukovsky and Samuel Marshak, and the much-loved poets of the youth, Yevgeny Yevtushenko and Andrei Voznesensky.

No doubt the fault for these gaps in our education was partly ours. Our resistance to the School's teaching was often because it was alien to us Brits and did not sit comfortably with our ideas on British socialism. On the other hand, the Soviet literary ferment engaged us as students of Soviet society of which we had become part.

I bade farewell to my two comrades, Steve and Roy, who returned to England in late 1962. Steve was subsequently to do odd jobs for the Party, working for the *Morning Star* and acting as secretary of a London Party branch. Like the Party, he drifted into gradual political oblivion during the 1980s, never having had a chance to apply his Moscow-learned talents to building communism in Britain. The other comrade, Roy Bull, fought to the end in various minuscule socialist parties, keeping faith in the revolution and no doubt regarding with dismay the demise of the communist dream in 1991. He died of cancer in 2005. None of us ever met up again.

As for me, at the end of the HPS course, I decided to stay in the Soviet Union, turning down a full-time Party post as organizer in the West Midlands of England in favour of a translating job in Moscow at Progress Publishers. Those Brummies don't realize how lucky they were, being deprived of my rabble-rousing talents. Actually, I have never been a leader of men, let alone women, and I'd have made a pathetic communist organizer. Moscow had not prepared me for bringing revolution to Birmingham.

One reason for staying on was that, as with students everywhere, my view of life around me was relatively blinkered, governed by the artificial life I had been leading. This was especially so within an elite political institution like the Higher Party School. During the course, apart from the 'grand tour' mentioned above, we had been taken to model factories and farms, even new high-rise housing estates like Cheryomushki in the south-west of Moscow – a district that the great Shostakovich had set to music, his operetta of the same name celebrating the optimism of a bright municipal future. We had not been exposed to the day-to-day realities and hardships of real Soviet workers and labourers. That was a closed world to us foreigners, the dirty laundry being washed out back, away from the front of house splendour we enjoyed.

Being a privileged foreign communist in the 'land of communism', I was handed tickets to watch the best ballet dancers in the world at the Bolshoi Theatre, enraptured by *Swan Lake, Sleeping Beauty, Giselle, Nutcracker, Spartacus* (I had never seen ballet back home). I attended poetry readings at the homes of the children's poets Kornei Chukovsky and Samuel Marshak, watched Chekhov at the Moscow Art Theatre. I mixed with the great and the good at glittering receptions. I recall the first anniversary of the Cuban revolution on New Year's Day 1962. This was a time when Soviet leaders were doing all they could to coax Cuba into the communist orbit. Although it now seems like one of history's inevitabilities, at the time I remember hearing that it was by no means certain that Fidel Castro would take the socialist road. So not only was the grand Sovetskaya Hotel with its glittering chandeliers, polished parquet floor and vast ballroom (once the scene of gypsy song and dance in the pre-revolutionary *Yar*, as the hotel was then known) hired out for the occasion, but a powerful line-up of political dignitaries occupied the high table: Nikita Khrushchov, President Leonid Brezhnev, foreign minister Andrei Gromyko and long-serving apparatchik, Anastas Mikoyan. The young Cuban Ambassador – he told me he was only 22 – must have been overwhelmed.

My friend and *Daily Worker* correspondent, Dennis Ogden, was an old hand at these dos and ensured we arrived early to bag a standing spot (everyone stood) near the bald, roly-poly Khrushchov. Thus it was I found myself within touching distance of 'Uncle Corny' (*Dyadya kukuruza)*, as he was popularly known for his hare-brained corn-planting schemes. To one side of me was a striking, silver-haired gentleman, bulky and with aquiline features. He was obviously partial to the Havana Club rum being handed round because he knocked it back as if there were no tomorrows. Soon he was flicking the bottoms of passing Cuban waitresses with his napkin. Noticing this, Khrushchov leaned across the table and grabbed my neighbour by the lapels. 'Do that again, Aram, and I'll give you what for! (*Ya tebe dam, Aram!*)' he shouted. Then, turning to me, he barked, 'Look after Aram, comrade!'

Wondering who on earth I might be, the swarthy man introduced himself curtly:

'Khachaturian.'

'Er, hello, I'm Jim Riordan, *anglichanin* – English.'

Then the penny dropped into my curious mind. Crikey! This was the famous Armenian composer of *The Sabre Dance*, *Masquerade*, the *Spartacus* ballet, the last of which I'd just recently seen the Bolshoi perform. Fortunately for me, he behaved himself and I earned a grateful smile from the boss.

When I look back, I smile guiltily. Here I was, an oik from Portsmouth, with no credentials apart from a Party card, chatting to composers, writers, even spacemen like Yuri Gagarin and the world's first spacewoman, Valentina Tereshkova ('Call me Valya and get me another vodka!'). As a young British communist, I was perhaps perceived as an oppressed worker, risking life and limb for the cause, fighting for the revolution. So I was someone to be encouraged, sympathized with, even envied. But not by all. Despite the natural hospitality of Russians, it was plain that not everyone shared their leaders' enthusiasm for propping up communist parties and regimes abroad at the expense of living standards in the Soviet Union.

But I was not only meeting Soviet celebrities. I was swapping music-hall jokes with some amazing Brits who'd traded in their navy-blue lion and unicorn passport for a red hammer and sickle one. Len Wincott, mentioned earlier, who had led the naval mutiny in Scotland in 1929 and spent eleven years in a Soviet labour camp; Donald Maclean and Guy Burgess, two of the most unlikely lads to turn up in Moscow of whom more later; my translator buddies George Hanna, Bernard Isaacs and Lennie Stoklitsky.

I had once asked Stanley Matthews for his autograph outside Fratton Park – my greatest football memory before coming to Moscow. Now I was meeting heroes of Russian football. If there was one footballer I longed to meet, it was the legendary goalkeeper Lev Yashin. In 1962 he was at the top of his form, though it wasn't until the World Cup in England in 1966 that he was recognized internationally as the world's best goalkeeper. In the late sixties I'd respond to a Moscow taxi driver's question of my background and straight back would come 'Ah, Bobbee Moo-oore, Bobbee-ee Charrrlton.' In response I'd say 'Lev Yashin', gaining an approving nod. Yashin was to receive many international awards, but when I met him his fame was mostly confined to Russian stadiums.

So in the belief that I could meet anyone I liked, I appealed to Friendship House: can you conjure up Lev Yashin for me? In no time at all, I was shaking hands inside the 'cockleshell palace' with the Dinamo keeper. He was taller than I had expected, a good six foot three inches, his dark hair brushed neatly back, broad-shouldered and as agile as a cat (he was known in the West as 'the black cat'). Not surprisingly (since he had grown up under Stalin and was, after all, a *dinamovets* – a Dinamo man, employed by the security forces and with an officer's uniform to match), he appeared nervous and cagey and, without taking off his fur hat and coat, suggested we take a walk in the snow. An odd suggestion in front of my colleague from Friendship House. I put on my own outdoor hat and coat, and we tramped the back-streets in the bitter Moscow cold.

Nothing very revealing came out of our conversation: he was born in 1930, father killed in the war when Lev was 13, mother struggled to bring up the family in Moscow, protégé of the Dinamo post-war goalkeeper 'Tiger' Khomich. I asked no 'leading' questions about his Dinamo affiliation – that would have been overstepping the rules (no one said aloud that Dinamo was sponsored and financed by the KGB). Years later, after his retirement, I was saddened to learn that he'd had both legs amputated, and died in 1990 at the premature age of 61.

Of the 1945 Dinamo team that came to Britain, I met the ebullient centre-forward Vsevolod Bobrov, now a well-respected radio commentator, and his fellow striker Konstantin Beskov who was to become a highly-successful coach with the army squad and the national team. Beskov had been involved in the strange circumstances surrounding the defeat of the Soviet national team on its Olympic debut in Helsinki in 1952. The shameful loss to Yugoslavia in the semi-finals came at a time of Stalin's break with Yugoslav communists, dubbed the 'bloody fascist clique of Tito and Rankevic'. Five of the Soviet team were punished by being deprived of their rankings and Beskov lost his title of Merited Master of Sport (and its accompanying remuneration). Later on, however, he was reinstated as the national team coach and looked after the side that beat Brazil 2–1 in 1980. Nowadays, he is lionized as the USSR's most successful manager. A man's fortunes in Soviet times could change with the wind.

There were times I'd wake up and pinch myself. Was it all a dream? How had I got here? A working-class kid from Portsmouth? What I couldn't forget was that I was living in a world still uncomfortably close to its terrible tragic past: purges and war, torture and execution. Millions, yes, millions, of innocent people had suffered. Stalin was only eight years dead in his glass coffin which I visited more than once in the Red Square Mausoleum before he was turfed out. At the same time, I was dreaming of the glorious future, of the day when communism would prevail all over the world. To an impressionable Pompey lad still struggling to take it all in and make sense of it, Russia was, as Churchill once put it, 'a riddle wrapped in a mystery inside an enigma'.

But unofficial excursions had revealed a darker side to Soviet life. For example, my wife had spent ten days in the nursing home with a Kremlin cook where Tania was born. Olga was a jolly lady who used to amuse the other mothers by spraying patterns on the wall with milk from her bountiful breasts. She and her husband, and sundry other family members, lived in a typical rural wooden house at Barvikha, a forty-minute ride on the *elektrichka* train from the city centre.

Annick, Tania and I enjoyed many a feast at Olga's and Vitaly's table. The couple, both Kremlin cooks, reminded me of the nursery rhyme about Jack Sprat and his wife: while Olga was languid and big in all proportions, Vitaly was a skinny little chap, full of nervous energy. His party piece was to produce a full bottle of vodka out of thin air just after I'd downed my half of the first bottle, when I thought I was safe.

In winter we went skiing with Olga's sister, Sveta, in the Russian forest with its towering fir and pine trees; in summer we gathered wild strawberries and mushrooms, scaring away elk and wild boar. Vitaly and I would flagellate one another with birch twigs in the near-stifling Russian bath-house before taking a dip in the bracing stream that ran through the village. Then back to the table for more ritual vodka drinking (down the hatch, no dilution), accompanied by lumps of fat, black bread, numerous side dishes (they were Kremlin cooks, after all!), beetroot soup, kebabs, *pelmeni* (little packets of mincemeat wrapped in pastry). Mmm. The only problem was that I was a sucker for taking up the Russian challenge to my British manhood and tried valiantly and foolishly to keep up with the toasts.

Before the hospitality took a hold, I did notice that the village possessed no gas or running water (they used the village pump). That was not unusual. What was surprising, however, was that the neighbouring dacha colony belonging to Party Central Committee members enjoyed all mod cons: gas, piped hot water, electricity, telephone. As with the earlier revelation about the perks available to Party bigwigs, this was another rude reminder that all was not as it should be in the land of social equality. That was not the only eye-opener in the village of Barvikha. The collective farm wheatfields had a bigger harvest of green thistles and dandelions than of golden wheat. Perhaps a latter-day Timofei Lysenko (Stalin's favourite farming geneticist – and a charlatan – one of whose schemes had been to rear herds of giant rabbits) was planning to make bread from thistles?

Had I returned straight home upon graduation with bright pictures painted on my mind, I might have joined the ranks of communists who saw only what they wanted to see in the 'land of socialism'. I would thus have done a disservice not only to the communist movement, but to the millions of Soviet people living in rural poverty and working the land in a collective and state farm system that patently did not function as it should.

I discussed my misgivings with other Moscow-based Brits, like the one-time spies Donald Maclean and Richard Dixon (aka Squires), an officer in the British Army who had switched sides in Berlin after the war, but since they had burned their boats and were stuck in Moscow they could, or would, give little advice. I was mainly alone with my confused thoughts; I would spend hours by myself, walking around Gorky Park, trying to figure things out and debating whether to hand in my Party card.

In the end I decided to stay on in Moscow and learn more about this contradictory society and its politics. So, in late August 1962, on completing my HPS course, I signed on as a translator at Progress Publishers. Translating, though a form of propaganda, did not strike me as compromising any principles or working against my native country, as spying might have. Not that anyone had invited me to spy at any level, at least not since I'd been cajoled by Her Majesty's Armed Forces into monitoring Soviet military aeroplanes in Berlin.

The vast Progress (recently renamed from the Foreign Languages Publishing House) building, located a couple of hundred yards from Gorky Park, on Zubovsky Boulevard, housed proof readers, editors, translators and sundry Party and trade union overseers in every language imaginable. Its overall boss was Sergei Pavlov, an erstwhile English interpreter who had worked for Stalin himself at the wartime Yalta and Potsdam summits with Roosevelt and Churchill. Maybe it was the strain of this experience that made him appear scared of his own shadow, with his facial tic that was hard not to imitate in his presence. He also had the disconcerting habit of repeating the last few words of your every sentence, like an echo chamber. Goodness knows what Stalin must have made of him.

I was allocated a two-bedroom flat opposite the University Metro Station in the south-west of town. The apartment was ample for the three of us, well equipped with all we needed (in the pre-TV era). Much to the disgust of my Russian friends I covered the parquet floor with sea-green carpet. Being above a fresh-fish shop and a hairdresser's, the flat always smelled oddly of live catfish and eau-de-Cologne.

I did my translation at home, working in my usual disciplined and fairly well-organized way on Russian-English translations of glossy magazines like *Soviet Union*, *Culture and Life*, *Sport in the USSR* and *International Affairs*, as well as books on philosophy and politics. God, the books were boring; the work rather like gnawing through a mile-long loaf of stale bread. On a visit in 2007 back to my old workplace I found the hallowed halls of Progress had been turned into a casino. Progress indeed! It brought home to me that my translations had been a complete waste of time.

Strange as it may seem, we English-speaking translators paid little attention to *what* we translated, apart from the genuinely interesting historical works, like those of Lenin, Marx and Engels (yes, we translated the Russian, not German, editions of their works into English!) With a relatively fresh pair of English eyes, I was lucky enough to be able to pick and choose my material, and whenever possible I plumped mainly for historical works, sport and children's stories and folk tales, which would later inspire me to become a children's author.

My fellow translators were a motley crew of English and American communists and fellow travellers, most of whom had come to the Promised Land before the war. A few were the children of White Russians who'd fled the Revolution; some of them had attended English schools in China and, in a fit of patriotic fervour, had emigrated to the Soviet Union after the war (it was also one of the few countries that would have them once they'd got their marching orders from revolutionary China) – only to end up in labour camps or temporary exile as potential spies! Several of my colleagues had tragic tales to tell. Lennie Stoklitsky, for example, had been brought to Moscow in his early teens by his American communist father and mother. Soon after, his father was arrested in the 1938 purges and executed; his mother committed suicide and Lennie remained alone at fifteen. He became an office boy at *Moscow News* and worked his way up to become a top translator. Despite having only one lung, Len used to run me ragged on the tennis courts beside the Lenin Stadium.

Working with such experienced and helpful people made me feel at home, and helped insulate me from the rigours of a society of hardship and political restraint. Since I earned ten times more than the average worker, my family could purchase more or less all we needed, although there was not a lot that money could buy apart from cheap booze, cigarettes, Cuban cigars (I didn't smoke the former, and Russians didn't smoke the latter), and drab clothes. Many times, even necessities like razor blades and toilet rolls disappeared from shop shelves. I remember asking Melinda, Donald Maclean's wife, please to bring a toilet roll with her when she came to dinner, as all my local stores had run out! The request didn't seem unnatural at the time – I could hardly have Donald or Melinda having to resort to pieces of *Pravda*! By the end of the month, I was often reduced to eating porridge when my cash ran out.

My social life was full, quaffing beer at the British Club of a Friday, going to receptions and rubbing shoulders with celebrities and Soviet leaders, watching and playing football. In many ways I lived the life of Riley (*not* Sidney Reilly, the Russian Jew who became known as 'Britain's Master Spy' in Russia at the turn of the 19–20th century!)

The one fly in the ointment was my marriage. While Moscow life suited me fine, Annick was becoming increasingly unhappy. She had no translation to divert her, very few friends to pass the time with and after the birth of our second daughter, Nadine, in July 1963, she now had two children to look after. After a year of my employment at Progress, Annick returned home to her parents in Picardy. She was to come back to Moscow less and less frequently over the ensuing years. My marriage was on the rocks.

Nadine had come into the world in an unusual way. With a month to go before her scheduled birth, Annick and I had a chicken supper with an Australian friend. The chicken was off and smothered in fried onions to disguise the smell. That night, both Annick and I had stomach aches that continued into the following morning. All the straining and gastric turbulence brought on Annick's labour pains; as she lay groaning on the bed, I phoned the hospital and called for an ambulance. One hour passed. Two hours. Still no ambulance. To my anguish and to the accompaniment of my wife's howls of pain, the baby's head crested, covered by a mop of black hair. Just as the tiny mite slid into my waiting hands, the doorbell rang. The paramedics! Saved by the bell! It was a close-run thing.

There had been another reason for my staying on in Moscow after the course ended at the HPS. I wanted to complete my research into Soviet sport for my doctoral dissertation I had started at my original alma mater, Birmingham University. The material I was unearthing was changing my (English) view of the role of sport in society. Far from being on the periphery, sport was pivotal in Soviet social development. After the revolution, sport had been accorded the role of being an agent of social change, with the state as pilot. Its utilitarian functions included promoting health and hygiene, military training, labour productivity, integration of a multi-ethnic population into a unified state, international recognition and prestige, all of which might feature under the tag of 'nation-building'. Further, partly under the influence of Marxist philosophy that stressed the interdependence of the mental and physical states of human beings, the Soviet state emphasized the notion that physical was as vital as mental culture in human development, and that it should be treated as such both for the all-round development of the individual and, ultimately, for the health of society. All this was a far cry from the dominant (aristocratic) concept in Britain of sport being separate from politics.

This enhanced state role and control of sport, however, had its sinister side; it had resulted in a phenomenon surely unprecedented in world sporting history: the arrest and execution of hundreds, perhaps thousands, of sports personalities. At the time the archives did not establish the exact number of victims. What was clear was that Stalin's paranoia and demand for purge quotas extended to leaders in all walks of life, sport included. As a result, during the thirties the purges carried off five sports ministers who had run Soviet sport, the Olympic Committee members for the Baltic states, the heads of the major sports colleges, eminent sports scientists and medics, and probably thousands of leading athletes. The fate of just one, Nikolai Starostin, is discussed in Chapter 11.

Like most other white-collar employees of Progress Publishers, I also joined the Spartak sports society – automatic membership came with my trade union dues. It cost me nothing and got me involved with Russians at play and so I took up playing tennis in the courts beside the Lenin Stadium and dabbled, badly, in the relatively new (to Russia) game of badminton with my good friend Yuri Sdobnikov (one of the ex-China English translators). But I still had a foot in the British sporting scene in Moscow, continuing to play each Sunday morning in the Diplomatic Corps kickabout. By now I was a veteran and captain of the UK and Ireland team, proudly leading them out against the only opposition there was, the Rest of the World team, still captained by the bare-foot Kenyan Ambassador.

One Sunday morning in early June 1963, I noticed a familiar figure on the touchline. It was my pal Gennady Logofet, the Russian right back who had kindly helped me with my doctoral dissertation. He was chatting to a slight, dark, wavy-haired older man. When Genna called me over after the game, he introduced me to Nikita Simonyan whom I knew to be the Spartak chief coach and one-time player for the club.

'*Molodets*' – 'Well played,' said Simonyan with a broad grin.

'Lucky you didn't tread on any bare toes with your big feet,' joked Logofet.

Some good old dressing-room banter. I was ready for more but what he said next completely took me aback.

'How'd you like to join one of our training sessions?'

Now, Gennady had already helped with my research by gaining access for me to the sports archives. This was a bonus. No doubt he had Simonyan's permission to make the offer.

'Er, fine. When?'

'Tuesday, ten o'clock. Tarasovka. Do you know it?'

I nodded. I didn't know it, but I had heard of Tarasovka as Spartak's training ground, north of Moscow, about an hour's train ride from Komsomol Square. I jumped at the chance of seeing Soviet football from the inside.

As a parting shot, Genna called, 'Bring your boots.'

I thought he was joking. Then it occurred to me that if I really wanted to research Soviet football I needed to see it from the inside, talk to players, observe the training methods and facilities. Gennady and Nikita Simonyan had obviously talked this over, maybe even asked permission from above – from Starostin or higher. I later discovered this to be true. As Spartak players would say, 'You can't spit or piss without the boss's say-so!'

Never in my life had I attended a training session of a professional football team. So I was more than a little nervous as the train from Moscow chugged into a fly-blown station outside Tarasovka. No one was there to greet me; it was still early, around nine o'clock, and I imagined that none of the others had turned up yet. On the platform was a solitary railway official sweeping dust with a bundle of goose feathers. I asked him for directions to the training ground, and then I set off on foot down an beaten-earth track in the middle of typical Russian countryside. After about half a mile I came upon an oasis in the desert: a modern, well-equipped sports training camp, complete with saunas, a medical centre, several watered pitches, gyms and changing rooms.

The camp was utterly unexpected and out of keeping with the surrounding rustic backwardness of thistle 'wheatfields', rumbling carts, empty shops and peasants who could have easily stepped out of Count Leo Tolstoy's estate of *Yasnaya polyana*, which was only a few miles down the road. On the other hand, this being Russia, all that glittered was not gold. The rusty showers in the changing rooms did not work, and the main training pitch was a bare, bumpy field with scarcely a blade of grass or chickweed in sight. This was the training ground and sports camp not only of Spartak, but also the national team, the best Russia could offer.

Then again, a warm sun was shining and who was I to carp? Unsure where to go or what to do, I sat on a bench outside the dressing room, dangling my football boots before me. Eventually, players arrived in ones and twos, along with a *massagist* – physiotherapist, team doctor (female) and two nurses, as well as the assistant coach, Nikolai Dementiev. One or two glanced at me in curiosity. My heavily accented response to a few customary hellos probably gave them the idea that I was from Latvia or Lithuania, certainly foreign, not from around their way. But surely it was too late in the season for transfers? No doubt my unannounced presence at the training ground would have made them nervous. A new face was not always a kind one in those days.

When the senior coach, Simonyan, arrived about ten o'clock, I relaxed. He would introduce me as a comrade from England who was researching Russian football, put an end to any lingering doubts as to what I might be doing there. When he invited me into the dressing room, however, Simonyan treated me as if I was a top-class international.

'Comrades, this is Yakov Eeordahnov,' he said with a wry glance in my direction. I didn't bother to correct him. In Russian, James is Yakov or Jacob. 'An English army team star.'

What? A star!? True, I'd mentioned to Gennady that I had played a few games for the British Army on the Rhine during National Service, but a star? Either he was taking the michael, or he really didn't know. I couldn't work it out.

Faces looked up respectfully, equating the ragtail BAOR team with the Central Army Sports Club, TsSKA. And thankfully, that broke the ice. Oh, so I was one of them, a *futbolist*. Not only that, an *armeyets*, an army man. A player. Well, at least until they saw me play. It soon became evident how rusty my skills were when I was included in the speed and strength exercises and in 'attackers v defenders' tackling. Luckily, Simonyan ended his little charade there and didn't expose me in the practice game that followed. Though my lack of fitness had let me down, my long legs and heading ability saved me from total humiliation.

While the players went for a rub-down and medical check-up, I thanked Simonyan and Logofet, had a wash in a cracked wash basin, returned my sweaty Spartak shirt and turned to go. No one congratulated me. That, I thought, was that. Sitting on my wooden seat on the train back to Moscow, I felt really chuffed. That beat hobnobbing with composers, politicians and spies by a country mile. A tale to tell my mates down the British Club the following Friday. I would put it top of my Moscow memories. But for the moment, I thought no more about it.

The following Sunday morning the phone rang at around nine thirty, just as I was leaving for our diplomatic kickabout.

'Yasha?' came a husky voice. It sounded matey enough, though misdirected phone calls were quite common in Moscow.

'Er, yes.'

'Nikita Petrovich Simonyan. Can you come to the stadium?'

'Ye-ess-sss.'

It was a very circumspect hiss of a reply. This could be a wind-up from the footman-barman at the British Club, or someone else putting on an Armenian accent. But I couldn't be sure and didn't like to be rude just in case . . . The next words knocked me back.

'Bring your boots. Two o'clock on the dot.'

It was definitely a Russian voice overlaid with Simonyan's singular Armenian accent.

The phone clicked.

If it was really Simonyan, why was he inviting me to the stadium, and with my boots? If he was helping my research cause by giving me a pre-match run-out on the Lenin Stadium turf, the gesture was a little over the top. It never entered my head that I would be playing!

First things first. My loyalty was to the British Isles and I was now late for the Diplomatic Corps match on the Lenin Stadium reserve pitch, two metro stops down the line at Lenin Hills. Grabbing my boots, white shirt and dark blue shorts, my blue and white socks, shin pads and a towel, I rushed off to catch the tube across the road at *Universitetskaya*.

The match started as usual with the Kenyan Ambassador rolling up in his black limo on to the grass verge, and his manservant striding out to place the ball on the centre circle. We had sorted ourselves out into two roughly equal teams before going at it hammer and tongs in a most undiplomatic free-for-all. Whether the mainstay of my team, the English, Irish and Scots, had indulged too much the night before I don't know, but we were sluggish and lost to a late goal scored by an Algerian equerry. Having done my duty to Queen and Country, I strolled the few hundred yards to the Lenin Stadium in my tracksuit, dusty and sweaty. I was directed to the home dressing room where a worried-looking Simonyan was pacing up and down.

One look at me must have deepened the furrows on his brow.

'You're on standby,' was all he said.

Standby?

Seeing my bewildered look, he explained, half to himself, 'Valery's sick. Seryozha's injured. I might play Igor, but we need height. I could have to pitch you in.'

Valery turned out to be the regular centre-half, Volkov; Seryozha was Rozhkov, and Igor the famous Netto. Though no one said so at the time, it transpired that Volkov had been 'bitten by the green snake' – i.e., in the nearest English equivalent, he was as pissed as a newt.

Simonyan was so preoccupied he didn't seem to notice how dishevelled I was, having just played a full game. I took my turn on the masseur's table, embarrassed by the dust and sweat I'd accumulated, hoping it would be seen as the result of an over-zealous warm-up. I got pummelled and kneaded like builder's putty and had knots undone where I never knew I had any. No one seemed to pay me much attention as Simonyan went the rounds of the team: he stood before each player sitting on the dressing-room bench, and spoke quietly and in some detail to them. Finally, he came to me.

'Don't let me down, Yasha. I've stuck my neck out for you.'

'I'll do my best,' I mumbled.

'None of your English rough stuff,' he said with a twinkle in his eye. 'Fair play.'

Russian, like most languages, has no equivalent of 'fair play', which he pronounced in English. I nodded.

'Stick closely to their centre-forward. Don't give him a centimetre. You're slower than he is, so stop him before he runs at you.'

'Yes, Nikita Petrovich.'

'That's all. Enjoy yourself.'

Enjoy myself? I was as nervous as a kitten. Not a single player had spoken to me, not even the normally garrulous Gennady Logofet. They were all preoccupied with their own preparation: stretching, running on the spot, kicking the brick wall, as well as pre-match rituals like combing their hair.

The physio threw me a neatly ironed Spartak shirt, shorts and socks; he saw I'd brought my own shin pads. The shirt had the number 5 on the back. In a daze I pulled it on; it was too small, but there were no bigger ones available, it hardly fitted into my white shorts.

The referee entered our dressing room before we left and, to my surprise, inspected the kit of each player, ensuring shirts were tucked in, socks pulled up to the knee, boots clean and laces neatly tied. He smiled at my short shirt and wished me luck: *Shchastlivo, synok* – 'Good luck, lad.' I don't know whether he realized he was talking to the first Westerner ever to play in the Soviet football league. If he did, it might have passed through his mind that, if the Stalinists returned to power, his life could be on the line.

The last person to talk before we filed out was our captain Igor Netto. They were certainly not words that would have graced an English dressing room. He apparently spoke, not as captain, but as Young Communist Secretary for the team. The speech went something like this: 'Comrades, we must at all times uphold the honour of Soviet football. To be a *Spartakovets* is to follow in the footsteps of the heroes of socialist labour and the brave Greek slave and revolutionary Spartacus. Play honestly and be an example to the younger generation.'

He didn't mention that I was playing because of the dishonourable conduct of the regular centre-half, Volkov, or that we were following in the footsteps of our brave manager Nikolai Starostin who had spent ten years of his life exiled to Siberia.

I later discovered that Igor Netto was a committed Party member, officially responsible for the morals of all Spartak players. He was chosen by the Party to present a documentary film of the wartime football match in Kiev played between local German servicemen and Soviet Ukrainians (the Soviet secret police invented a heroic story which they infamously titled 'The Match of Death'). Netto must have known he was colluding in deceit. But he had his own guilty secret. His brother, Lev, was a dissident of Estonian background who had been arrested and exiled under Stalin. The presence in the Spartak team of a 'representative of capitalist countries' could not have pleased Igor. He seemed to avoid looking at me during his 'pep-talk' and, during the match, rarely passed to me. Perhaps as compensation, as we left the dressing room, a few of the players patted me on the back, saying, *Ni pukha, ni pera* – 'No down, no feathers' = 'Good luck'. To which the obligatory answer is *Kchortu!* – 'Go to the devil!'

We lined up in the tunnel alongside our opponents wearing white shirts and shorts, waiting for the stadium technician to switch on the familiar football jingle – a jaunty patriotic march tune. Then out into the sunshine at five to four, marching in step, side by side with the Tashkent team, led by the referee and his linesmen in the British-invented black uniform.

How did I feel?

Nervous. Unbelieving. In a dream. I barely saw the 50,000 or so spectators; I dimly heard the muffled roar. Did they notice me? Since programmes were as haphazard as team sheets, the fans depended on the stadium announcer for line-ups. I don't recall hearing my name, but someone afterwards said I was introduced as Yakov Eeordahnov, replacement for Volkov. Shame. How much more exciting to hear: 'Comrades, this is Dzhim Reeordan, an English army international from Portsmouth, making his first appearance for Moscow Spartak.'

It has to be remembered that this was 1963, only a decade since Stalin's death and the anti-foreigner campaign, a couple of years since the removal of the tyrant's corpse from the Mausoleum, and less than twelve months since the Cuban Missile Crisis when the world was teetering on the brink of

The Moscow Brits: Len Wincott is sitting far left. Hilda Perham is in the middle in the check dress. In the middle row on the left, with his arms folded, is Tom Dexter. Behind Dexter is Robert Dalgleish and myself.

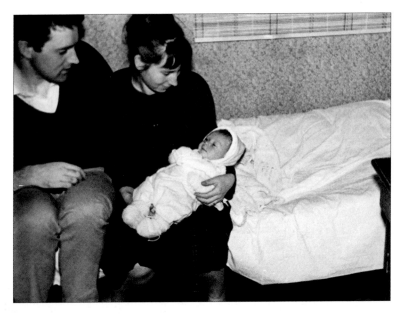

Annick, Tania and I in our hostel room at the HPS, 1962.

With daughter Tania outside the HPS, 1962.

Moscow winter in front of the HPS, 1962. Razor blades were in short supply.

With Young Pioneers, the Soviet version of the scouts, in Moscow, 1962.

With Roy Bull at the Young Pioneer Club, singing 'Old Macdonald had a farm', Moscow 1962.

At a Young Pioneer Camp
in Armenia, 1962.

Socialising with other young communists around a bonfire in the woods outside
Moscow. Steve, the one-time milkman, and I are far left.

Comrade Dave Cohen and I at the chief Moscow synagogue, 1961.

A group of British comrades doing some sightseeing, in front of St. Basil's cathedral on Red Square, 1961.

At the unveiling of the Karl Marx statue: Khrushchov is stood next to the leader of the GDR, Walter Ubricht, 1962.

With the Moscow Dinamo keeper and greatest Russian player of all time, Lev Yashin, in 1964.

At the time of my debut for Spartak (with my daughter Tania) on the reserve pitch beside the Lenin stadium (pictured in the background).

PHOENIX

JIM RIORDAN

MOSCOW SPARTAK 1962-64

FIX '65

Footballers
OPEN SERIES

'Famous' footballers were featured on cigarette cards in the sixties. God only knows why I'm in stripes!

With doting fans, in Cuba, 2005.

nuclear war. Though I was unaware of it at the time, it was only eighteen years since British communists living in Moscow had been arrested and sent to forced labour camps in the frozen wastes of Siberia. No one knew whether there would be a return to the past at any time, including another xenophobic campaign, the hounding of foreigners and Jews (with my new name I qualified as both). Simonyan and those running Spartak were taking an enormous risk in playing me, even if I was a communist. But this was a *time of risk*, of pushing the boundaries in all walks of life, with Khrushchov and the new Soviet leaders trying to liberalize post-Stalin society and gradually open it up to the world. All the same, there was no point shouting my presence from the rooftops.

Our opponents that day were Pakhtakor, from the Uzbek city of Tashkent, in Central Asia. Instead of small, nut-brown Uzbeks, the Pakhtakor team consisted mainly of blue-eyed, fair-haired Slavs with a smattering of Armenians.

Spartak that day put out a team that must have resembled the following (I am relying on a 2001 handbook):

Maslachenko

Logofet   Eeordahnov   Soldatov

Korneyev   Netto (captain)

Ambartsumyan   Reingold   Falin   Sevidov   Khusainov

I remember lining up, but not knowing exactly where to stand. Netto came to my rescue. Like a sergeant-major, he barked, *Stoi v seredine* – 'Stand in the middle'. In those days, a centre-half stood like a sentinel in the middle of the defence, ahead of the full backs, but slightly behind the half backs. Having taken up my position, I was able for the first and last time during the match to look around me at the sprawling crowd around us. In the front row stood the soldiers ringing the stadium, facing the fans in case of trouble – not that I'd ever seen any in Moscow. Beyond the uniformed guards were the spectators sitting on concrete seating that rose up and up into the vast blue sky. In those days the Lenin Stadium seated up to a hundred thousand people. Such happy, smiling faces full of anticipation. I couldn't let them down; after all, I was one of them, a fan plucked from the terraces allowed to grace the hallowed turf.

Straight away, I noticed a gaping difference between the crowd at the Lenin Stadium and the ones I was used to back home at Fratton Park. Here there were no shirts or scarves in team colours, no rosettes, no rattles or bells. Fearing any 'bourgeois extravagance' that might light and fan nationalistic fires, the authorities had banned them from the stadium. In the absence of private enterprise, making and trading in badges, scarves and flags, supporters had to make do with chants, songs and the 'second' Russian language known to all as 'prison slang'.

One surprise to me was that I was standing not on grass, but on freshly-watered curly weeds with the occasional tiny white flowers sitting on the dusty soil like an ill-fitting toupe on a bald head. I'd played on better surfaces in the Portsmouth Dockyard League. Although it was late afternoon, it was still very warm, full of the dry Moscow heat that saps your energy and catches in your throat. The strong, fresh aroma of chickweed hung in the air, intermingling with the swampy smells of the river that flows past one end of the stadium – not by chance was this once the site of the British River Yacht Club.

High above the terraces was a single concrete VIP box, which looked at that great height like an airborne bunker. It was built so that no one could see the occupants, and fans never knew which dignitary might be blessing us with his or her presence. The self-professed 'Friend of All Sportsmen', Josef Stalin, had always cultivated his image as a remote godhead, far removed from such earthly pleasures as football. The current Party boss, Khrushchov, despite his attempts to be *vox populi*, eschewed all forms of popular sport except chess, while the President, Brezhnev, though a football fan, avoided public exposure after someone took a pot-shot at him as he drove from the Kremlin in an open car. I therefore never knew who was witnessing my debut from on high.

The referee's whistle broke into my reverie. We kicked off towards the Lenin Hills (now 'Sparrow Hills') end. Right away, our No. 9, Falin, slipped the ball to Valery Reingold who turned back towards his own goal and passed along the ground to me. I could not have been more grateful. In typical Riordan fashion, with no one closing me down, I lumped the ball upfield. At least I didn't miskick and land on my backside. Netto was far from satisfied. As the ball sailed over the goal-line, he hissed, 'Pass to a man, not the crowd!'

Despite his moaning, that one kick so early in the game seemed to boot out the collywobbles from my stomach and give me confidence which increased when I headed the ensuing goal-kick hard and true towards the left wing and Khusainov controlled the ball and set off down the wing. At the sight of the crowd's favourite on the attack (with my assistance!), the crowd began to buzz with excitement.

I'd always wondered whether the roar of fans could be heard on the pitch. Now I knew. Shouts, screams and chants all became diffused into a buzz rather like a swarm of hornets circling round your head. But the fans' hum soon fades away and normally subsides into a groan. So now as the winger's cross was caught by the Pakhtakor keeper.

One minute had passed, only 89 left for me to shine or disgrace myself. The next few minutes were to demonstrate to me the difference between a professional match and our Dipcorps games just a few hundred yards away. Once again the ball came high in the air towards me. Easy. I didn't even have to launch my beanpole frame off the ground. Yet, just as I was about to head the ball, a hefty nudge knocked me off balance and I missed the ball completely. 'Referee!' Not for the first time in my career, I discovered how unfair life is for us big men. Lean on a shortie and you risk being sent off. Push, kick, tug a lofty and the referee turns a blind eye, as if a foul evens up the difference in size.

Luckily, my 'error' led to nothing more than a corner. 'Right, matey,' I told the centre-forward under my breath, 'if you want to try a Tommy Lawton on me, I'll be ready this time.' But the ball flew over our heads to the far side of the goal where their right winger hit a shot that found its way through a tangle of legs and into the far corner of the net. 1–0 to the Uzbeks. I could hardly be blamed for a goal that came from the wing and not my central patch – my mistakes, or lack of, was how I usually judged my performances.

Not that the crowd saw it that way. The team was collectively responsible for conceding a goal to the unfavoured team from the deserts of Uzbekistan, and the fickle fans soon let us know with a chorus of piercing whistles. At the time, English fans did not whistle their displeasure; they booed. I can vouch that an ear-piercing crescendo of whistles is more disconcerting than a chorus of boos. That stung Spartak to step up the tempo, at times no quicker than walking pace, a sort of stop-go waltz rhythm: slow, slow, quick-quick, slow, typical of the fairly isolated Russian game of the early sixties.

We launched attack after attack, keeping the lion's share of possession. I would have gone up for corners, as was my habit, had not Netto signalled me to stay back. It was just as well because, midway through the first half, with the tall Logofet out of position, the ball was played down their left wing and a fleet-footed attacker raced unmarked over the half-way line. I was caught in two minds: either to stay close to my centre-forward (as Netto had instructed) or to leave him to block the winger's run. I chose the latter option, backing off and hoping one of my own men would get back to intercept the cross.

I made the wrong choice. The winger cut inside and, with me backing off, let fly from the edge of the penalty area. Although our keeper, Maslachenko, got a hand to the ball, it went into the net off the angle of post and bar. Oh dear: 2–0 to Pakhtakor, and we were only midway through the first half. I could see that Netto was furious with his defence, though he kept his feelings to himself. Mind you, as a defensive midfield man, he was as much to blame, being caught upfield, as the rest of us.

The fans let us know how they felt. So angry were they that I thought the soldiers might have to shoot a few *pour encourager les autres*! If you've ever heard the sound of starlings twittering at twilight, multiply that by a thousand or two and you will have some idea of the ear-blasting whistling of Spartak supporters.

No matter how hard and often we attacked, we were unable to put the ball into the net. Since the play was now almost totally confined to our opponents' half, I was not exactly run off my feet, though just before half-time their nippy centre-forward collected the ball in his own half and ran at me. I was the only defender between him and the goalkeeper. The thought of bringing him down never entered my head; that was never my game. I backed off and backed off as he turned this way and that, trying to throw me off balance. Finally, as we reached the edge of the penalty area, I slipped, letting him past. With just the goalie to beat he chose power instead of guile and hit the ball past the post. What a let off!

The referee's whistle blew, as did 50,000 mouth whistles, and we trooped off for our wedge of orange and cup of tea – except that oranges could not be had for love nor money, and tea came in glasses with no milk. The mood in our dressing room was, to put it mildly, sombre. In silence we awaited the coach to raise our spirits and dole out advice. He was not a hurler of tea glasses. Quietly, patiently, he spoke to each player – in such a whisper that I couldn't catch his words. When he came to me, he shifted a towel and sat down beside me.

'You're doing well, Yasha,' he murmured. 'The goals weren't your fault. Stay tight on their No. 9. When you head the ball, lean into your man and jump above him, using your arms to launch yourself. I want you to win every ball, *ponyatno* – Got it? Every single ball. *Umnaya golova nogam pokoi dayot* – A wise head gives the feet a rest,' he said, paraphrasing the Russian saying that 'a stupid head gives the feet no rest'. *Molodets* – 'Well done.'

No ranting and raving, no criticism. Just sensible advice. In the manner of a Ron Greenwood or Alf Ramsey.

Whether it was the glass of hot tea or Simonyan's psychology I can't say, but when we ran out for the second half we felt confident we'd get the two goals back and go on to win. I soon put the coach's advice to good use by towering above an opponent to head the ball clear, only to hear the ref's whistle for a foul. From the resulting free kick I again got my head to the ball to clear the danger. I could almost feel the coach smiling in satisfaction.

Midway through the second half, Slava Ambartsumyan broke away down the right, beat the full back and, much in the manner of the post-war Portsmouth mercurial winger Peter Harris, pulled the ball back from the by-line into the path of the fair-haired Reingold who hit it low and hard into the corner of the net. 1–2. No hugging or kissing. Just a few delighted handshakes.

We piled on the pressure, searching for the equalizer, but it was beginning to seem as if it was one of those days when nothing would go right. I was growing desperately tired, puffing and panting like an old steam engine. It was bad enough trying to keep up with the pace of this game, but two matches in one day was far beyond my endurance. All the same, with time running out, Netto summoned me to go forward for a corner. I trundled upfield and stood as ordered on the penalty spot. What a glorious end to my debut it would be if I were to score. I'd go down in the history books (though that wasn't certain – the goals of Torpedo's disgraced Eduard Streltsov had been expunged from the records!) and be a 'hero of socialist labour'.

Over came the corner, my defender missed it and all I had to do was nod the ball into the gaping net. It all happened so quickly. In my excitement, I missed the ball completely with my head and it flew wide off my shoulder. Groans all round. Whistles from the fans.

Eeordahnov na mylo! 'Riordan's neck for a soaping!'

My blushes were saved by a last-gasp penalty given, unfairly I thought, for a trip on Yuri Falin. Reingold tucked the kick away into the top corner. 2–2.

I can't say if I was more glad or sorry to hear the final whistle. I was a touch sorry that I hadn't given a better account of myself, but that disappointment was mitigated by the fact I hadn't made too many boobs and let Simonyan, my team-mates and the Spartak fans down. One thing's for sure. I was dead tired. My legs felt like lead, my head throbbed and my tight stomach muscles now betrayed the nervous tension of the match that I hadn't felt during the game. I was dead on my feet but at the same time I'd never felt more jazzed. I'd just played in front of 50,000 at the famous Lenin Stadium. As that realization started to sink in, a wide smile crept across my face. Then, looking around the dressing room, I knew I'd have to put my own personal celebrations on hold. I was the only one smiling. The furrowed brow of the coach, the downtrodden looks on my team-mates' faces and the still echoing whistles of the fans told me this was not all a jolly stroll in the park, a joyful run-around. Too much depended on it. We'd drawn a game we should have easily won. My excitement gave me away – perhaps I wouldn't make it as a professional footballer after all . . .

Football was a serious business. For our opposing team, Pakhtakor, it was to prove fatal. At the height of the 1979 season, suddenly, and without explanation, the team vanished from the league without fulfilling its remaining fixtures. It was not until twelve years later, in 1991, that the authorities revealed that there had been an air crash on the team's return home from a match in the Ukraine. Altogether, 178 passengers and crew died in the accident. No one survived. The dead included thirteen members of the Pakhtakor team I played against.

One consequence of the drawn match that was concealed from me was payment. The fiction prevailed that all Soviet sport was amateur, a charade that began when the Soviet Union joined the Olympic movement in 1951. So the appearance had to be given that all the top players were either students or in the armed and security forces, playing for the joy of the game and the pride of their institution. Of course, I knew my team-mates received large sums of money from the Sports Committee and under-the-table payments from sponsors like the Moscow City Council, but I didn't wish to embarrass them by asking for remuneration. Stupidly, I didn't even ask if I could keep my shirt – or even a sock – as a souvenir. It was years later, on my return to Moscow to record a BBC radio documentary, that I was awarded my Spartak shirt.

I dragged my aching bones into the communal pool and let my body soak out its tiredness. While lying in the tepid water, Gennady Logofet kindly invited me to join him and some others at a Russian bath-house. Thinking it rude to refuse, I dried off and piled into his car with three others. We sped off out of town to a wooden house not far from the writers' colony of Peredelkino. I can't remember whose dacha it was – a high-ranking army officer, I think – but we were expected and the bath-house at the end of the garden had been readied for our arrival. After stripping off we each grabbed a birch-twig besom tied with twine and entered a fug of dry steam. My four colleagues climbed on to a higher bench, while I sat on the lower until I had accustomed my naked pink body to the heat.

Every so often, our host would empty a wooden bucket of water infused with *kvass* – fermented rye – over the heated stones. The smell of the *kvass* and the birch twigs was intoxicating. It was not long before I climbed up to the higher level and joined in the mutual flagellation with the birch leaves. Logofet told me it would help to open up the pores and swish the blood round the body, and I had no reason to distrust him. So I became acquainted with what Tolstoy and others referred to as uniquely Russian: the wonderful, invigorating steam of the Russian *banya* or bath-house. Unlike Tolstoy, however, we did not jump from the *banya* into a bracing stream or roll about in the snow.

While in the bath-house our host supplied us with cool bottles of Czech beer – true ambrosia for parched throats and bellies. But that was just the prelude to the ritual yet to come. Having opened our pores and slaked our thirst on *pivo* – 'beer' – it was time for a snack. We adjourned to the main house where the hostess had generously prepared a table of hors d'oeuvres: salami, herring and raw onion, salmon, caviar, sturgeon in aspic jelly, black bread, pickled cucumber and mushrooms and goodness knows what else. The food served as nothing more than blotting paper for the bottles of little water (Russian for 'water' is *voda*; so *vodka* is 'little water').

This ritual feast, I was told, was as much part of playing football as kicking (or, in my case, heading) the ball. It was our sacred duty as *Spartakovtsy* to demonstrate our vodka drinking capacity. We had to show our *muzhestvo* – a mixture between 'courage' and 'manhood' – by keeping up with our co-imbibers. I would gladly have declared myself a cowardly weakling if I could have got away with it, but Logofet slapped me hard on the back and reminded me that I was one of them now. Thank you. Down the hatch. 'To victory!' 'To honourable draws!' And so on to oblivion. Playing football for Spartak requires more than football skills.

Through the haze I remember Logofet arguing that *stukachi* – 'informers' – like Netto never drank, that the 'old man' (Starostin) was a teetotaller and didn't like his players indulging. 'But all Russians drink,' he assured me, 'that's why they're Russians!'

Once again, I didn't think it polite to remind him that I was only present because one player, Volkov, got so stewed before a match that he was incapable of walking straight, let alone kicking a ball. As it happens, I still had a hang-over when I reported for training, as instructed, on the Tuesday morning. Logofet and the other three seemed as right as rain.

I trained as a fully-fledged team member for the rest of the week, Tuesday to Friday, 10–12 and 2–4. The first part of the day concentrated on fitness and ball skills; the second consisted in watching a black and white film (not easy when both teams seem to be wearing the same kit!) of the previous match, analysing mistakes under the coach's guidance and working on tactics for the next game – away to Ararat of Armenia. As it turned out, I was not included in the team for that match. Simonyan took the trouble to explain that it was too risky exposing me to the volatile Armenian fans. 'Not that I've anything against Armenians,' he said with a grin and an exaggerated Armenian accent. 'But you'll play again, I promise you.'

He was as good as his word. A few weeks later, when I was already beginning to think I was a one-hit wonder, he called me over during a Friday training session and asked how I felt about playing on the coming Sunday. I said I'd be delighted. Same place: *Stadion imeni V.I.Lenina* – 'The Lenin Stadium'. Same time: kick-off 4 p.m.

So old 'Eey-or' donned the No. 5 shirt again in the same line-up as against the team from Tashkent. This time our opponents were Kairat of Alma-Ata, capital of the mainly desert republic of Kazakhstan, not far from the border with

China. In the early part of the war, potential trouble-makers, like Volga Germans, Koreans and militant Muslims from the Caucasus, like Chechens and Ingush, had been rounded up and dumped in the wastes of Kazakhstan to prevent them joining up with the advancing German armies. It was hardly surprising, therefore, that the core of the Kazakh team was made up not of Islamic Kazakhs, but Volga Germans, descendants of the yeoman farmers brought to Russia by the 'westernizing tsar', Peter the Great, in the early 18th century.

Spartak had already beaten Kairat 2–0 away from home, and having won two on the trot at home with easy victories over Kishinev of Moldova and Torpedo of Kutaisi (Georgia), were now vying with their perpetual rivals, Moscow Dinamo, for the league championship. So we couldn't afford to slip up against a relatively weak team like Kairat. It was, I suppose, a measure of Simonyan's trust in me that he included me in the team over a now fit and sober Volkov.

For me, the fact that I was a one-match veteran did nothing for the butterflies in my stomach, marching out to the familiar *tum-tum, tiddle-tiddle, tum-dee-dum-dum* of the pre-match jingle. As before, the coach had given each of us a quiet piece of advice, while the ever-serious Igor Netto had delivered his pep-talk. I noticed that few paid Netto much attention; some continued chatting throughout his moralizing. This might not be a reflection of attitudes towards Netto; the same had happened at the Higher Party School when eminent communists had come to give us a talk.

When we all shook hands in the centre circle, I observed that the opposing No. 9 was a big, burly, balding fellow with cross eyes. I don't know what his eyes had to do with his foot-balling ability, but they did lend him a sinister air and, for me, frightening appearance. Despite his bulk, he was surprisingly fast and agile, giving me the run-around right from the start. He was also adept at barging and backing into me and making it tough to strip the ball off him. If the substitution rule had existed in those days, I might well have been pulled off and replaced by Volkov. But, barring injury, the team was stuck with me for the entire ninety minutes. Russians aren't as polite as English fans, or as tolerant of mediocrity, and they gave me the bird in piercing waves of whistling. My confidence drained away. What was amazing was that the man I was marking never scored. Luckily, his skills did not extend to accurate shooting. Our inside-right, Valery Reingold, scored the only goal of the match during the second half which took us to the top of the league. Eventually, we were to finish runners-up to Moscow Dinamo.

That was my last appearance for the first team; I was demoted to the reserves, then gradually forgotten. The call never came again. Oddly, the more I played after that, in Russia or England, the worse I performed. Eventually I ended up, in my mid-forties, in the eighth division of the Portsmouth Dockyard League. How the mighty had fallen! Did any of those rough, tough dockies realize they were playing against a one-time *Spartakovets*? They certainly showed no respect for reputation or age.

Some 25 years after my appearance as a brief statistic in Soviet football, I ran into the legendary Igor Netto, my one-time team-mate, at Portsmouth's Alexandra Park, where he was playing as a regular for a team of Russian veterans. Few of the fifty-odd onlookers recognized or had even heard of the sixty-four-year-old as one of Russia's, and the world's, greatest footballers. He recognized me without much enthusiasm, asking no questions about my football career. He was as serious, taciturn and slim as ever, a teetotaller, dedicated to his craft. I asked him what he remembered of my Spartak performances.

'You weren't fit enough,' he said bluntly, adding, 'fair in the air, slow on the ground.'

He was quite right. It being the Gorbachov era in Russia, I turned the conversation to politics, asking Igor what he thought of *perestroika*.

'Not much,' he replied. 'Russians need a strong hand. Gorbachov is risking our socialist gains.'

He was right again. Gorbachov was to bring the entire communist edifice tumbling down with his policies, not least because he undermined all the hard-line communist leaders in eastern and central Europe. Although many Westerners praise Gorbachov for his boldness, he is generally reviled in Russia by both right and left.

I was surprised to hear of Igor's death just five years later; he had seemed indestructible to me. In a sparkling career he played 367 times for Spartak between 1948 and 1966 and captained the Soviet national team fifty-five times between 1954 and 1963.

In 2005 I made a radio programme with the BBC about Alexei Smertin, one of the first Russians to play in England (for Chelsea, Portsmouth, Charlton and, latterly, Fulham), and myself as the first Englishman to play in the Soviet league. I was looking forward to meeting up with my erstwhile team-mates back in Moscow, though I had a few misgivings. No one who has bridged the vast chasm between communist and capitalist times in Russia has been left unscathed by the traumatic impact it has had on society as a whole. Many ordinary Russians have rejected the communist past in toto and are ashamed to talk of their own part in it. In place of the 'moral code of the builders of communism', launched by Khrushchov, they now turn in droves to the medieval liturgy and ritual of the Russian Orthodox Church. Others, however, are still heedlessly nostalgic for the relative security of the 'good old days', when the Soviet Union stood tall in the world. I wondered on which side of the divide I'd find my old team-mates. It didn't take long to find out.

In preparation for the show, I telephoned my old pal Gennady Logofet to tell him I'd be coming back to Moscow. As with most of my old friends, I'd lost touch with him in the intervening years and we hadn't spoken for over forty years. That was the first shock. He claimed he could not remember that far back – owing to his short-term memory. At first, I thought he was joking. Then I wondered whether, like many 'New Russians', he was angling for a dollar sweetener. But no, nothing of the sort. He just didn't want to talk. I was hurt and bamboozled. When I tried to arrange a meeting in Moscow, he said he would be out of town in May when my visit was planned. I tried phoning other players, and found much the same response. They mostly quoted medical reasons for memory lapse or simply refused to talk about the past. None actually denied playing alongside, in front or behind me. Just 'I don't remember that far back', reiterating what Logofet had said.

One or two maybe, but not an entire team!

Later, in May 2005, when I arrived back in Moscow, I was invited by Boris Dukhon, Chairman of Spartak Supporters Club, to watch an indoor five-a-side match. A Spartak factory team from the Moscow suburbs was playing against another local Spartak team. Unlike in my era when traditional summer soccer gave way to winter ice hockey, the trend now seemed to be towards all-year-round football, with the indoor game also attracting well-paid foreign, particularly Brazilian, stars.

Dukhon told me that while few old players now went to the main stadium, some still congregated in the smaller, covered arena to talk over old times, especially when, as now, Spartak was in contention for the league championship. In the covered arena I was introduced to another old team-mate, Slava Ambartsumyan. I would not have recognized the one-time flying willowy winger had Dukhon not pointed him out to me. This pot-bellied, grizzled old-timer with hangdog features was just a shadow of the man I used to know. On introducing myself, Slava showed no signs of recognizing me (why should he if I didn't recognize him?) or remembering the past at all. He initially rambled on about strokes and Alzheimer's, his divorce and shabby treatment by coaches. Then, abruptly, he said, 'I don't want to talk.' When I jotted down my phone number and tried to press it on him, he refused to take it.

What the hell was going on? Did they fear Westerners deriding them for 'collaborating' with the communist regime? Perhaps their past was a private world shared only with relatives and close friends of the era? Interestingly, they were coming to the indoor stadium for a five-a-side encounter watched by a hundred or so people, and had never stepped inside the open (now 'Olympic' rather than 'Lenin') stadium which they had once graced. Perhaps indoors, in the more intimate atmosphere of a few hundred or so mainly youthful fans, they could pass unnoticed and mingle with old friends. Outdoors, in the stadium with which they were associated, they might encounter older football supporters who would recognize them, bring up the past, try to recapture old times they wanted to forget. The phenomenon is not unknown among ex-professionals in England. I recall seeing George Best, a friend of the then Portsmouth owner Milan Mandaric, in the corporate lounge at Fratton Park in 2005; he would fly all the way from Ireland to the south coast of England for the pre-match conviviality, then often not take his seat in the Directors' Box to watch the game.

Subsequently, Russian journalists told me it was quite a common affliction in Russia – the 'Russian past syndrome'. As for me, I was beginning to feel embarrassed before my BBC producer, Mark Burman; I could see doubt in his eyes. Had I made the whole thing up?

Then, on the path from the indoor arena to the Olympic Stadium, I suddenly saw in front of me a stocky, white-haired figure. Khusainov! My Spartak team-mate and left-winger of forty years past. Although I had not seen him for over forty years I recognized him at once. 'Galimzhan,' I called, catching him up. He turned, stared into my face and murmured, 'Dzhim, *zdravstvui*!' His eyes lit up in genuine happiness to see me. '*Skolko let, skolko zim?*' – 'How many summers, how many winters?'

We embraced as warmly as if Spartak had just scored against Dinamo. Before we could say another word, however, an elderly woman, evidently his wife, pulled him away, explaining testily, 'He's not well. Had a stroke. Understand?'

I dropped back, hugely relieved to be recognized, but saddened by the news about one of my heroes, the Tatar Spartak captain after Netto and great favourite with fans, known to all as *Khusainchik* – 'Little Husain'. The Spartak handbook tells me he played 346 times between 1961 and 1973, gaining thirty-three caps for his country. I had the honour of sharing two of those Spartak games with him. Now I had another reason to be grateful. Thank God for

Galimzhan Khusainov! I had started to wonder whether I really had dreamed it all. Not only the football, but the entire extraordinary experience of Moscow in the early 1960s.

All the same, it is sad to think that players of the period are ashamed and weary of their past. Soviet football in the sixties was certainly not free from scandal and mendacity, but it was a far cry from the corrupt, oligarch-run, money-dominated Russian game of today. Back then, it provided welcome enjoyment for many, many thousands of ordinary Russians who saw support for their team as a temporary escape from the political rigidity of society. It was precisely that quality of Spartak that enabled a far from gifted lad from Portsmouth to play, proudly, for the team.

Strangely enough, I too have had a reticence about speaking about the past. It took me a couple of decades to even mention it to anybody and over forty years to write about it. I find it difficult to explain. Just as two of my British comrades who studied with me in Moscow in the early sixties cannot openly admit to having studied at the Higher Party School, I have long been guilty of a silence about my political apprenticeship and my playing for Moscow Spartak. Perhaps it is because I regarded the Soviet Union as another world, separate from the one we live in now. It is a past shrouded in secrecy that it is best not to unveil. With the passing of communism in Europe, that separateness, that secrecy has gone too. I may not like what has taken its place, but at least it has removed the barriers that have obstructed the fond memories of my past.

10

LONG SHADOWS ON MOSCOW GROUNDS

Football was not the only game played by the British residents of Moscow. There was one sport which, like football in the 1870s, was exclusively English: cricket. British diplomats had brought the game with them when they settled in Russia, just as they did in India during the Raj. In 1868, before the advent of football in Russia, the British, as mentioned earlier, had founded the St Petersburg Cricket and Lawn Tennis Club. Although tennis spread far and wide – until it was damned as 'bourgeois' and fit only for the 'white pants brigade' by members of the proletarian culture movement in the 1920s – cricket along with croquet, which invariably accompanied it, did not catch on among the locals; perhaps it was never intended to. The problem was as much climatic as cultural, since snow covered the Russian wickets for half the year. Rotten luck!

Undaunted, a hundred years on, in the early summer of 1963, an intrepid band of Englishmen set out to resurrect the game of cricket in 'some corner of a foreign field' outside

Moscow. The initiator was Donald Maclean. Not that he owned as much as a bail or a ball; they were not high on his packing list when he had fled to Russia in a hurry twelve years before, having been unmasked as a Soviet spy infiltrating the Foreign Office. His *idée fixe* had long been to transfer the sward of the green cricket fields of Cambridge to the dried shrub-land of Moscow. Through one of Guy Burgess's English friends who was a frequent visitor to Russia, the MP Tom Driberg, he ordered six stumps, four bails, a cricket ball, two bats and one set of pads. In the event three stumps, no bails, an old cricket ball, one bat and one pad (in slightly soiled condition) arrived.

That was encouragement enough for Maclean to take his plan further. All he needed now were players. No amount of persuasion could tempt Burgess to face a cricket ball; the most he would agree to was umpiring. In those Cold War days there was no question of inviting 'the other side' – the diplomats, journalists and students – to make up the numbers. Neither British nor Soviet officials would have sanctioned a jolly get-together of reds and blues. What would the readers of the *Daily Mail* say if they saw a picture of the 'traitor' Maclean running out Our Man in Moscow, even if they did share the same public school and Cambridge college, and were both members of the Reform Club?

It was weird. In many ways, the diplomats – those who represented Her Majesty in Moscow and the spy duo who had defected – had more in common than they had with the embassy skivvies or us communist hoi-polloi. They spoke with the same accent, had attended the same top private schools and colleges, laughed at the same jokes that the rest of us found unfunny, reminisced on middle-class and esoteric sports like croquet, real tennis and squash, admired the same prose and poetry – of Chesterton, Kipling, Waugh and Tennyson – and even walked with that same confident swagger. If they had come upon each other naked, in the bath-house, they would surely have felt blood brothers, belonging to a privileged fraternity whose membership was denied to the vast majority of the population.

So the cricketers had to be Moscow residents, which meant communists and fellow travellers (non-communists who sympathized with communism). This narrowed the choice somewhat. Now, however odd it may seem, we used to have regular *Daily Worker* bazaars at which money was raised for the newspaper's 'Fighting Fund' to keep it afloat. Communist Party membership was on the wane after the twin blows in 1956 of the Soviet invasion of Hungary and Khrushchov's revelations about the Stalinist purges at the 20th Party Congress. These Moscow bazaars were often held in her flat by the indefatigable Hilda Perham, whose husband had recently died in Moscow; she stayed on, sending her young daughter to a Russian school. Hilda gave us a sense that we were doing our bit for the Party back home.

Many Moscow exiles were keen to take part, baking cakes, making jam and cordials, and selling old English memora-bilia. A more diverse and colourful group of charitable contributors could scarcely be found: from a London taxi driver and an ex-sailor, who had both come to the 'promised land' in search of the communist dream, to former scions of the British Establishment, like Maclean, Burgess and, later, Kim Philby. Burgess often turned up at the bazaars hoping for a jar of home-made marmalade or his favourite seed cake. Even politics was something few of us had in common, especially considering that the air was sometimes shared between comrades who had spent ten years in labour camps and those who had ratted on them.

It was at one of the bazaars that Maclean started rounding up potential cricketers. Some of his original plans, such as us all being decked out in white, soon had to be ditched since no Moscow shops sold white flannels or jumpers, just white industrial overalls that no self-respecting Eton and Cambridge man would deign to wear. Eventually, fifteen enthusiasts volunteered. They included four or five translators, like myself, a handful of Russians who had attended British public schools in China and emigrated to Russia after the war, and erstwhile intelligence agents: besides Burgess and Maclean there was Richard Dixon (aka Squires) an officer in the British army who had switched sides in Berlin after the war. Although the average age was over fifty (Maclean was fifty, Burgess fifty-two) and no one had played for years, no cricketing team could have sallied forth with more collective vim and vigour.

A reasonably flat, grassy area was located beside the dacha of Robert Dalglish. Goats had nibbled the grass to passable stubble, not county level perhaps but no worse than I'd seen at some football grounds, like Spotland in Rochdale. Admittedly, Spotland wasn't covered in cowpats which proved hazardous when fielding and slowed the ball down considerably in the outfield.

Melinda, Donald's American wife, and a few other wives had made some cucumber and caviar sandwiches; and plenty of Czech beer awaited the players. The scorer was former *British Ally* editor Archie Johnstone, who sadly died soon after of a heart attack during a Volga cruise. The *Daily Worker* correspondent Dennis Ogden captained the younger seven-man team, the Players, while Donald Maclean captained the other, eight-man, outfit, the Gentlemen.

Despite his enthusiasm for the game and his great height (six foot five), Maclean proved inept with both ball and bat. We had dispensed with wides and the LBW law, and so Donald planted himself squarely before the stumps and swiped viciously at everything that came his way. He was finally run out (of wind as much as anything else) for an inglorious fifteen. He would have been out earlier if the umpire had kept his eye on the game instead of the Czech beer, and hadn't kept wandering off for a drink.

My own batting contribution was minimal since my second ball hit a divot and skidded along the ground – a daisy cutter – under my flailing bat. Out for a duck. To cries of 'Bad luck, old boy', the one-time RAF Junior Technician (one stripe upside down), Lofty Riordan, gave way to the erstwhile Army sergeant-major (three stripes right-way up), George Hanna. Ironically, the Players were made up of other ranks and sundry riff-raff, while the Gentlemen had once been officers in the armed forces or school cadet force. In a way, we were keeping the class flag flying high in a corner of a foreign field.

Although we Players were a man short, we scraped enough runs together (fifty-four, I recall) to beat the Gentlemen with one wicket to spare. To the chagrin of the losers, the winning runs were scored by a former American spy who adopted a baseball stance and clipped Maclean's bowling clean over the wicket-keeper's head and down to the boundary. A Yank beating an Englishman at his own game. Maclean wasn't best pleased.

As we cricketing pioneers trooped from the wicket, soaked in sweat, happy and exhausted, Maclean led polite clapping for the winners, shouting, 'Three cheers for the Players, hip-hip-hooray, hip-hip-hooray, hip-hip-hooray!' A touch of old-fashioned English etiquette to round off surely one of the most unusual and unlikely sporting events ever to grace a Moscow pitch.

Moscow contained a fairly small British communist community, so it was not difficult for everyone to know everyone else. But since many had had a chequered background – camp inmates, informers, spies and ex-journalists who'd jumped ship – it went without saying that you did not ask too many questions of your 'comrades'. You just accepted them as 'one of us', however different their social background. Within our British enclave, no one could have been more different or led such amazing double lives as Guy Burgess and Donald Maclean.

Guy Francis de Moncy Burgess was born in 1911 into a well-to-do naval family. At thirteen he went to Eton, then on to Dartmouth College for two years until poor vision disqualified him from a naval career. He returned to Eton and, in October 1930, went up to Trinity College, Cambridge, to read history. At university, he was, according to contemporaries, a brilliant scholar, an engaging conversationalist and voracious reader (his favourite fiction was Jane Austen and George Eliot). He felt liberated here, away from the stuffy confines of public school life and not only did he make no secret of being gay, he flaunted his homosexuality. As the biographers Bruce Page, David Leitch and Phillip Knightley note in their *The Spy Who Betrayed a Generation* (Penguin Books, 1969), 'Cutting a swathe from Trinity to King's, bellowing with laughter in the Hall, parading a pair of sixteen-year-old "nephews" along the banks of the Cam, he became one of the best-known figures in the University.'

Donald Duart Maclean was born in 1913, the son of Sir Donald Maclean, a non-conformist, deeply devout Liberal MP who led his party for three years. At fourteen, Donald went to Gresham's public school at Holt in Norfolk and then, in 1930, to Trinity College, Cambridge, to read French and German. Like Burgess, he plunged into public communist-led campaigns and, in 1933, told his mother, Lady Maclean, that as soon as he had finished with Cambridge he was going to Russia as a teacher to help with the revolution. Around the same time, he wrote an article in *Communist Left*, in which he argued that capitalist society 'is doomed to disappear'. Soon after, however, he made no more public utterances on communism, appeared to abandon his former political allegiance, and settled on the rather strange choice of a career at the Foreign Office. How they ever let him in is beyond me.

Their Cambridge friend Kim (Harold Adrian Russell) Philby was born in 1912 in the Punjab to an Indian Civil Service father, Harry St John Philby. Kim went to Westminster School and, in 1929, went up to Trinity to read history with economics. For Philby, the turning point in his political life was the 1931 general election when the Labour government under Ramsay MacDonald was roundly defeated, yet MacDonald continued as Prime Minister at the head of a so-called National Government with no socialist policy or principle. Many socialists regarded this as a betrayal of all the Labour Party stood for. Not for the first time, they felt, Labour had let them down and betrayed the working class. Kim had campaigned for Labour at the election, yet never committed himself to print. He wrote no articles and signed no speeches.

While at Cambridge all three, with their colleague Anthony Blunt (later knighted, he was Surveyor of the Queen's Pictures and Drawings until 1978), became dedicated communists.

As an international and world-renowned seat of learning, Cambridge was not insulated from the turbulent world politics of the 1930s and the onsurge of fascism. Many of its students recognized the struggle as being between the opposing ideologies of fascism and communism and some took it upon themselves to get involved directly.

A communist cell was formed at the university in 1932 which set about recruiting members for the British Communist Party. Private cell meetings were attended by two Marxist academics at the university – Maurice Dobb, an economist at Pembroke College, and J. D. Bernal, a crystallographer who was considered the finest young scientist at the university. Thanks to the Communist Party's standing in the international vanguard of art and culture, they could also attract many of the promising young artists, poets, novelists, playwrights, actors and musicians at the university. James Klugmann, Maurice Cornforth, Julian Bell and Charles Darwin's great-grandson, John Cornford (the last two were both killed in the Spanish Civil War) all joined up. Klugmann and the promising young poet Cornford, both undergraduates at Cambridge's Trinity College, were to become two of the British Communist Party's leading intellectuals and members of its Executive Committee. The poets Cecil Day-Lewis, Stephen Spender and W. H. Auden also joined the Party.

Burgess, Maclean, Philby and Blunt decided they could promote communism more effectively by infiltrating the cloistered corridors of the Establishment, not through openly attacking it in print. At some time around 1933 or 1934, they seem to have been recruited as spies for the Soviet Union. It has never been established as to who exactly signed them up (they never told me!) and why precisely these four Cambridge

Marxists – rather than Klugmann or Cornford for instance. In his introduction to the book *The Spy Who Betrayed a Generation*, the spy specialist and novelist John le Carré poses the question: 'Recruited by whom?' and cannot answer his own rhetorical question: 'Between the ages of 19 and 21, it seems, these children of Cambridge were recognised, courted and consciously seduced into a lifetime of deceit. By whom?'

All we know, and it has been incredibly well documented since, is that they became spies for the Soviet Union. By 1934, they publicly eschewed Marxism and, with their solid upper-class credentials, began to pursue careers in Establishment institutions such as the Foreign Office, the BBC and MI6 (the Secret Intelligence Service). Their employers welcomed them, keen to recruit from their own class, evidently conflating their social background with implicit loyalty to King and Country, assuring themselves that secrets were safe with their own people. When Burgess was arrested for importuning in a public lavatory, he had only to give his word as an old Etonian and Cambridge man for the judge to find him not guilty. The 'club' does not elect liars or traitors, ergo an old Etonian or Cantabrigian can not be a liar and never a traitor. Many years later, when the British Ambassador in Washington, Sir Archibald Clark Kerr, was warned by the CIA that the Embassy contained a 'mole', he assured the Americans that it could only be someone 'below stairs' – a 'cleaner, footman or valet'. As one-time communist and secret agent Malcolm Muggeridge put it in his collection of writing, *The Infernal Grove* (London, 1973), 'A ruling class which is on the run, as ours is, is capable of every fatuity. It makes the wrong decisions, chooses the wrong people, and is unable to recognise its enemies – if it does not actually prefer them to its friends.'

The three Cambridge friends, Burgess, Maclean and Philby, became the most successful and, to those they spied against, the most notorious, agents in history. As the US Secretary to the Army, Wilbur M. Brucker, said in 1956, 'Burgess and Maclean had secrets of priceless value to the communist conspiracy.'

By the end of the Second World War, the three could hardly have been better placed. Kim Philby was head of the Soviet section of MI6 and, in 1949, became first secretary at the British Embassy in Washington and MI6 liaison officer with the newly created CIA. He therefore was able to expose all the anti-communist conspiracies sponsored by Britain in Eastern Europe and show the Russians that Britain was conducting anti-Soviet activity operations even while we were close allies in early 1944.

Donald Maclean served in the Washington embassy in the section dealing with the Anglo-American atomic energy programme and he was able to provide the Soviet Union with information on the joint American and British atomic energy project. As a result, Russia was able to break the US monopoly of the atomic bomb (and all the blackmail and bullying that went with it) years before the West expected (the USSR tested its first A-bomb in August 1949).

Guy Burgess became secretary and personal assistant to Hector McNeil, Minister of State for the Foreign Office, in 1946, and then went to serve in Washington. Before he left the US capital (in disgrace, following drunken and openly homosexual affairs), he was told by Kim Philby, with whom he was staying, to alert Maclean to the fact that MI5 was on to him – but that in no circumstances was he to defect with Maclean. For some reason, Burgess ignored the latter and, with Soviet assistance, he and Maclean escaped to Russia in 1951. Maclean was thirty-eight, Burgess forty.

After the disappearance of Burgess and Maclean in 1951, suspicions surfaced about a 'third man' and Philby's name was frequently mentioned privately as the person who had tipped off the two diplomats that the Secret Intelligence Service was on to them. Philby's name could not be mentioned publicly until a Member of Parliament, Colonel Marcus Lipton, did so under protection of parliamentary privilege. Colonel Lipton's naming of Kim Philby as the 'third man' in 1955 drew an emphatic denial not only from the 'outraged' Philby (who summoned journalists to his mother's house to declare his innocence), but also from the then Foreign Secretary Harold Macmillan. It was to be another eight years, in January 1963, before Philby's name was mentioned in Parliament once more, this time after his defection to Russia. Edward Heath made a short statement to the effect that before defecting Philby had confessed to having been the 'third man'. There was a strong suspicion that it was less embarrassing to the British government and the Foreign Office to let Philby go than to open up a can of worms in a treason trial.

Once in Moscow, Philby refused to meet Burgess, even when he was dying, referring to him as 'that bloody man'. All the same, when Burgess died, he left his friend a third (£2000) of his estate, perhaps out of remorse for betraying his cover (it did not escape MI5's notice that Burgess had lived with Philby's family in Washington).

Guy Burgess never really settled in Moscow. He never learned Russian, refused to use his Russian alias or knuckle down to a job. I met him a few times, usually at funeral wakes (it was not uncommon for British communists to come to Moscow suffering from a terminal illness – in hope, perhaps, of a miracle socialist cure) for people like Archie Johnstone, the editor of *British Ally*, or the long-serving *Daily Worker* journalist Ben Francis. On my one visit to Burgess's modest and untidy apartment, he met me in his blue silk pyjamas and delighted in showing off a whole drawerful of Old Etonian bow ties and the tailor's tag on his bespoke suits from Eton High Street.

Rather oddly, having learned that I was from the naval town of Portsmouth, he reminisced about the 'sailor boys' he'd known, the nights he'd spent with them at the Keppel's Head Hotel down by the Hard, and his sexual activities in the Queen Street red-light district. He laughed at memories of the 'Aggie Weston Sailors' Home' which had rigged up nets above the cubicles so that sailors could not climb over into the neighbouring bed.

'Those nets never deterred *me*,' he said with a guffaw. The only other geographical location we had in common was the lovely Hampshire village of West Meon where Mum and I used to go bluebelling in springtime and blackberrying in autumn. Guy's memories were more personal – of his family's country house nearby and services in the old West Meon church. I recall his last words to me, with a wistful sadness in his eyes: 'One day I'll return to West Meon.' And he would, albeit after his death.

He invariably smelled exotically of alcohol and tobacco intermingled with garlic and cloves, which he would pop into his mouth from a side pocket as if they were chewing gum. His fingernails were bitten down and yellowed with nicotine. Once an extremely handsome man, tall and broad-shouldered, he was now stooping, podgy and concerned about his health. When I last spoke to him at the cricket match, he said, as mischievously as ever, that his doctor had told him to refrain from sexual intercourse . . . 'but Tolya just won't understand'. Tolya was his live-in lover (though he also had an Alsatian dog of the same name!).

A month after his erratic umpiring, he left his sixth-floor flat overlooking the Novodevichy (New Maiden) Nunnery (to his annoyance, within earshot of the Lenin Stadium roar!) and checked himself into the Botkin Hospital. He died just a fortnight later, on 30 August 1963, of acute liver failure and thrombosis. He was only fifty-two.

Guy Burgess was quintessentially English and regarded himself as an extremely patriotic Englishman. When I once dared to ask why he had betrayed the country he loved, he seemed lost for a reply. 'You know, James,' he finally said. 'I never betrayed my country. I love England passionately; but I have nothing but contempt for those who threaten to ruin it – fascists in the thirties, the Americans today. They are the ones I despise.' A characteristic toss of the head dismissed any further questions.

Although he never said as much, it was apparent that he had no intention of paying lip service to the Soviet political line of the day, or accustoming himself to Russian culture, even that of the Moscow intelligentsia. But having made his bed, he had to lie in it. Guy was the archetypal upper-crust Englishman, accustomed to buttered toast, marmalade (Old Oxford) and a strong cup of tea, from a teapot, for breakfast. Russians did not do toast, make marmalade or drink tea with milk (in any case both the tea and milk somehow tasted different from the English variety). His nostalgic quoting of the one-time Cambridge student Rupert Brooke betrays his longing for a disappearing rural and academic England: 'Stands the Church clock at ten to three? And is there honey still for tea?' More sombrely, he'd quote Brooke's *The Soldier*, 'If

I should die, think only this of me: that there's some corner of a foreign field, that is for ever England.' Not, perhaps, the England he'd run away from, more a Utopian aristocratic vision of days gone by.

Somehow he seemed to think he could transfer his eccentric, droll persona to a Moscow that was plebeian, largely drab, deeply suspicious of foreigners (the vast majority of Russians had never met any, except in war), especially those who made no effort to adjust. Guy's dry and often caustic sense of humour was never understood by Russians and his jokes would usually go down like a lead balloon. I don't believe that during his spying career he ever contemplated the reality of living in Soviet Russia. The natural Moscow antidote for him was to seek solace in the bottle, which he did with a vengeance. As an excuse, he was fond of quoting the poet John Keats, 'That I might drink, and leave the world unseen, And with thee fade away into the forest dim.'

There was little chance of him leaving the world unseen with Russian minders and British journalists constantly on his tail. His silent protest was to walk down Moscow's main thoroughfare, Gorky Street, wearing an Old Etonian tie and his Order of Lenin medal. He once described Moscow as boring, 'like Cambridge in the long vacation'. It was certainly an improvement on his first Russian town, Kuibyshev (now Samara), where he and Maclean had been sent for their first two years in Russia to keep them out of sight of potential assassins or British newshounds, which he described as 'a vision of hell. Can you imagine Glasgow on a Saturday night in the nineteenth century?'

Guy's exotic story did not end with his death. At the funeral, Maclean and I were the front pallbearers followed by men like Dennis Ogden, almost a foot shorter than the pair of us. As we walked down some steps, we felt something shift in the coffin, and Maclean whispered, 'I wouldn't put it past the old bugger to sit up and cry, "Ah ha, fooled you all!"' Once inside the crematorium, a double bass and violinist played 'The Internationale' high on a balcony as a speech was made by a high-ranking Party member of the Central Committee over the coffin lying on a stone slab. I can never hear that rousing tune now without thinking of the bass and fiddle scraping away in that freezing crematorium.

Unusually for Russia, the coffin lid was screwed down (so giving rise to rumours that Burgess had shot himself); the distraught Tolya (the lover, not the dog) suddenly dashed forward to prise off the coffin lid, at the same time as Burgess's brother, a naval commander in full uniform who had flown over for the funeral, tried to hold it down. Just at that moment, someone pulled the switch and the coffin started to descend into the depths. It took several of us to pull them both to safety in the nick of time.

The next day we were enjoying Guy's well-stocked drinks cupboard and drinking his health when his brother arrived with the urn and a bemused smile on his face. 'I never dreamed,' he said, 'that one day I'd be walking down Gorky Street with Guy under my arm wrapped up in a copy of *Pravda*.'

As a postscript to Burgess's death, forty-three years later I visited the beautiful, sleepy village of West Meon in Hampshire that he'd spoken so fondly of, having learned that his ashes had been interred in the Burgess family plot in the graveyard there. I finally located the grave and found it overgrown with feather grass and burdock. The inscription reads:

IN
LOVING MEMORY
OF
GUY FRANCIS
DE MONCY BURGESS
DIED 30 AUGUST 1963

A more idyllic last resting place for a self-proclaimed patriotic Englishman could not possibly be found.

Tall and distinguished, holding himself very upright like a guardsman, Donald Maclean was much more sociable than Burgess and did his best to fit into the Russian way of life. He was helped immensely by the arrival in September 1953 of his wife Melinda and their three children (two boys and a girl). He learned Russian, adopted an alias, Mark (Melinda became Natasha), and worked for the Soviet Foreign Ministry, specializing in Western economic policy, on which he wrote a book published in Russian.

He and Melinda/Natasha came over to my place for dinner a few times, with Donald ever eager to practise his fluent French with my wife Annick. Looking back, I'm somewhat puzzled about why our conversation never went beyond life in the Soviet Union or, indeed, about the dreadful crimes of Stalin. Not once did it stray to past, present or future in Britain or, indeed, France. No one had to draw the line and say, 'Look, these are the forbidden topics.' There seemed to be an unspoken rule at all our get-togethers that you never mentioned a person's past – unless they brought it up themselves. That applied as much to British comrades unfairly imprisoned, like Len Wincott and George Hanna, as it did to our 'illustrious' diplomatic spies. Since Donald and his

American wife Melinda had no interest in football, dinner table conversation consisted mainly of tittle-tattle about life in Moscow, our children's schooling, Khrushchov's attempts at loosening the stays of rigid Soviet society, the latest Russian literary works, strikingly conventional.

I must say honestly that I found Donald Maclean, as my mother would say, the perfect English gentleman. There were just two eccentricities that perhaps gave some truth to the unpleasant rumours about his weakening mental condition and lack of gratitude to the Russian Secret Service mentioned by his Russian handler in London, Yuri Modin, and others who have written about him. Both might be understandable if you are facing possible execution and living a double life as a top British diplomat and a spy for the Russians. In the more relaxed haven of Moscow I noticed no obvious mental problems.

The first was that he could not hold his drink. It is all relative, of course, to who is trying to force it down your gullet and contesting your manhood. People react in different ways to inebriation. I become just plain silly and embarrassing. Some grow maudlin. Others turn nasty. Donald was of the latter disposition. At one of our dinner parties, Donald was one moment his normal self, politeness personified, the next he was unaccountably rude and offensive. It was as if he'd sipped a phial of Dr Jekyll's medicine. It came as an awful shock, like hearing a priest suddenly let loose a string of expletives. We'd finished a delicious suckling pig (a rare treat in Moscow – or anywhere else for that matter) and were just starting on the dry, tasteless Russian cheese. Whether I'd committed some faux pas of etiquette I don't know (as a one-time waiter I would hope not), but all at once the public school mask slipped and I was treated to as ripe a riposte as

I've ever heard from Portsmouth dockies on the football terraces. Surely I must have misheard . . . Did he really call me a 'stupid c . . . ' and a 'f . . . . . . moron'? That was mild by contrast to the words he used towards my wife.

How much more titillating this anecdote would be if I had clocked him one and spilled the beans to my *Daily Mail* chum, Keith Moffatt. I can see the headlines now: 'Communists in drunken brawl over a bit of cheese . . . ' 'Maclean in punch-up with drunken red!' Nothing was further from my mind. I was still in a state of disbelief as Melinda hastened to help him on with his overcoat and fur hat, before hustling him out of the door, with apologies. Donald himself never apologized. In all probability he didn't remember his outburst the next morning.

Other Muscovites talked of his drunken binges, drying out periods and hiding of bottles at home. It is possible his excessive drinking drove his wife Melinda into Philby's arms on the latter's arrival in Moscow in 1963. They spent three years together before she returned to Donald.

My impression of Melinda was of a very beautiful woman in her late forties, ever polite and kind, a caring mother; she was especially close to her only daughter, also Melinda. She was more friendly with the other English-speaking women in Moscow than she was with the Russians, and did not speak the language well. Not once did I hear her voice an opinion on politics; the idea that she was a closet communist all along is piffle. Back in England you could imagine Melinda organizing church fêtes or being a care worker for the less privileged. After her husband's death, she returned to her birthplace in America.

The second of Donald's oddities was that he would suffer no criticism of the Soviet Union. I remember once arguing with him about capital punishment (abolished in Britain, but very much in use in the Soviet Union) which he defended to the hilt. 'And yet thousands, if not millions, of innocent Soviet people have died,' I said. 'That is the revolutionary imperative,' he responded in justification. Strange: if the Soviet Union was for it, it seemed, Donald was too. That apart, I must say truthfully that I found Donald Maclean a polite, caring and charming person, even if we did come from opposite ends of the class spectrum.

He died in 1983 at the age of seventy. As with Burgess, his ashes were brought to England to lie alongside those of his mother and father. Strange that both Maclean and Burgess, committed and daring communists, returned to their aristocratic roots after their deaths.

I never met Kim Philby; he kept himself to himself. 'I have come home,' he declared on arrival in Moscow. There was no media coverage of his defection in Russia, nor did our British communist community ever learn that we had a new comrade in town. None of us had access to foreign news-papers, apart from the communist press like the *Daily Worker*, *l'Humanité* or *l'Unità* – and they kept quiet. In any case, the adventures of British diplomatic spies, Philby especially, were largely unknown to us; somehow their doings were not things we wished to know about. Philby himself, unlike his two cloak-and-dagger comrades, never tried to socialize with other ex-pats, apart from, that is, Maclean's wife! He also took up with another double agent who kept his distance from us – George Blake who, after being unmasked in Britain, was sentenced to 42 years in gaol in 1961, but escaped to Moscow five years later with the help of the Soviet Secret Service.

The fact that Philby followed on from Burgess and Maclean a dozen years later seems to indicate a reluctance to defect and abandon England for good. Not because he had any sentimental attachment to British culture, unlike his two comrades, but because he seemed to thrive on intrigue and enjoy the secret world in which he operated. Once in Moscow, he worked as a KGB adviser, lecturer and trainer of spies. He died in 1988 at the age of seventy-six, requesting that he be buried in Moscow. He was given full military honours in the Kuntsevo cemetery where a red marble gravestone records his military rank and medals.

There was much about Burgess, Maclean and Philby I would never comprehend. For a start, my commitment to Marxism and the Soviet Union was somewhat at odds with theirs. As young men, they had pledged themselves to a country they had never visited, to an ideology they had not studied in its practical application and to a regime that even abroad was dangerous to serve. They had remained faithful to that commitment, leading a perilous double life, for over thirty years in Burgess's case, over forty in Maclean's, and over fifty in Philby's. There is no evidence that they ever had any doubts or that they agonized over the purges or venal aspects of Soviet life, even after the illusion became a reality.

If someone like me, outside of the Establishment, was aware of Stalin's crimes and the communist repression in countries like Hungary and Czechoslovakia, revealed not only by Western scholars like Robert Conquest in his remarkable book *The Great Terror* (Oxford University Press, 1970), but by Soviet leader Khrushchov at the Twentieth Party Congress in 1956, it is certain that Philby would have known. In Britain, over a third of British communists left the Party in disillusionment following the Khrushchov revelations and the crushing of the Hungarian uprising in the same year. I suppose the radical difference between us was that Philby and his two friends were engaged for many years in espionage. Once a spy, always a spy. There's no escape. Few spies have been able or allowed to quit; those who have often ended up with a bullet in their brain. I could criticize all I liked, with a British passport in my pocket and the protection of Her Majesty's Government (whatever their distaste for my communist leanings). My Cambridge comrades had burned their boats, so were no doubt loath to bite the hand that fed them. For them there was no possibility of going back, except in an urn.

In a way they never took leave of the upper-crust world they were born into. They enjoyed the privileges of the Establishment, its institutional cosiness and security, its superiority, even arrogance. They did not need to spy for money even if their principles had allowed them to. They were idealists committed to the cause.

What their story makes abundantly clear is the role of privilege in British society, and the degree to which mythical blue blood and irrelevant marks of social and economic status, accent, clothes, manners, old school and university, could all be mistaken for evidence of political acceptability and superiority. The guilt, if there is any, should lie as much with the British class system as with the three men who exploited its snobbish delusions.

11

THE AMAZING LIFE OF NIKOLAI STAROSTIN

The person most responsible for my inclusion in the Spartak team was Nikolai Starostin, former captain and later the club's general manager. A tall, lean, bespectacled man in his sixties, he was always to be found at his office desk, impeccably turned out in suit and tie. The buck, as they say, stopped with him. So if there had been any ructions over allowing a debut to a foreigner, his head would have been on the chopping block. But, then, Nikolai Petrovich Starostin was used to taking difficult decisions . . . and paying the price.

Gennady Logofet once told me with regard to my doctorate on Soviet sport, 'If you want to know about Soviet football, ask Nikolai Petrovich. No one knows better than him.'

But would he give me the goods?

I'd been warned, *sotto voce*, that Starostin had done time, but that he had been pardoned or, as the regime liked to put it, 'rehabilitated'. He and his three brothers. It was common knowledge that the government had not allowed him to release his amazing story for public consumption. Not that his lips were sealed, however. Gennady Logofet often complained that in the dressing room the players had to put up with his endless stories of camp life and hardship.

The beginning of the sixties, up to Khrushchov's removal as leader in October 1964, was a period of social and political thaw, after the frosty atmosphere of the Stalin era, and extended to all areas of Soviet life, including football, as my unique inclusion in Spartak's team testified to. Outside of sport, it saw the publication of literary works that would never hitherto have seen the light of day including those of the monarchist, conservative Fyodor Dostoyevsky and the once-persecuted poets Marina Tsvetayeva and Osip Mandelshtam.

In 1962, a middle-aged former gulag inmate, Alexander Solzhenitsin, managed to publish his short novel *One Day in the Life of Ivan Denisovich* in the magazine *Novy mir* (telling of twenty-four hours in the life of a construction worker in a labour camp). For the first time the authorities were allowing writers to tell of life in the gulag. Moreover, a young generation of poets – Yevgeny Yevtushenko, Andrei Voznesensky, Bella Akhmadulina, Robert Rozhdestvensky, as well as the bard Bulat Okudzhava, set a new critical tone and conducted readings that could fill a football stadium with audiences sometimes reaching the 15,000 mark. In a way, the poets were the Soviet equivalent of the Beatles and Rolling Stones in the youth revolution sweeping contemporary Britain.

While Solzhenitsin could describe the camp life of a *fictional* construction worker, Starostin knew he could not write about the *real-life* experience of a footballer as well known in Russia as Stanley Matthews, Tom Finney and Raich Carter were in England. Football, evidently, was too popular for such a harrowing story to be *safely* set before the public. It was not until 1973 that Nikolai's younger brother, Andrei, who shared his fate, was able to publish his autobiography. Even so, he could make only veiled reference to the missing decade:

'People's destinies varied in the war years. Life took its toll. But when I returned to Moscow in 1954, *after several years beyond the Arctic Circle*[my emphasis] the capital was already building a new life.'

It was only with Nikolai's own (untranslated) autobiography, *Futbol skvoz gody* (*Football Through the Years*), published in the mid-eighties amidst Gorbachov's openness (*glasnost*), that the full truth came out. By then, after several visits to Nikolai's home, I knew the story, though I'd promised not to write about it until after his death. And since he lived to the ripe old age of ninety-four (or ninety-eight, according to some sources – he himself never knew), this is the first time I've written down his truly remarkable tale.

In Stalin's Russia of the thirties and forties, 'traitors' and 'spies' – the equivalent of 'reds under the bed' – had to be found and exposed everywhere, including within the world of football, to account for the defects in society. As Robert Service attests in his book *A History of Twentieth-Century Russia* (Harvard University Press, 1997), state violence was nothing new:

> Nearly a million Soviet citizens languished in forced-labour camps and colonies of the OGPU (secret police) by 1933, and further millions were in prisons, deportation camps and camp resettlement areas. Consequently, the Great Terror of 1937–38 was not a thunderclap in a cloudless sky, but the worsening of a storm that was already raging.

By the end of the 1930s, all of Lenin's Politburo had met their deaths at the hands of the only survivor, Josef Stalin; as much as 70 per cent of the 17th Party Congress in 1934 had been arrested and shot, and fifteen of the sixteen Red Army commanders, as well as tens of thousands of officers, were executed in 1937 on charges of espionage. By 1939, nearly three million people were in forced labour camps and prisons. As with the British communists living in Russia and the ongoing campaign of xenophobia, the purges did not end there; they continued after the war right up to Stalin's death in 1953.

Throughout this period vans and lorries with the innocent words *KHLEB* ('Bread') or *MYASO* ('Meat') printed on the sides day and night would carry victims out to the forest around Moscow where long, deep pits had been secretly prepared to hide the bodies of executed prisoners. Sometimes the condemned were tortured until they 'confessed' to their crime. The case file on the innovative theatrical director Vsevolod Meyerhold still contains a letter he wrote from prison to the Prime Minister Molotov:

> The interrogators used force on me, a sick, 65-year-old.
> I was made to lie face down and beaten on the soles of my
> feet and my spine with a rubber strap . . . When those parts
> of my legs were covered with extensive internal bleeding,
> they again beat the red-blue-and-yellow bruises with the
> strap and the pain was so intense that it felt like boiling
> water being poured on the sensitive areas. I howled
> and wept from the pain . . .
>
> When they added the 'psychological assault', as it's called,
> the physical and mental pain aroused such an appalling
> terror in me that I was left quite naked and defenceless . . .
> When I lay down on my bed and fell asleep, after 18 hours
> of interrogation, in order to return in an hour for more,
> I was woken up by my own groans . . .

> 'Death, Oh surely death is easier than this', the tortured
> person says to himself. I began to incriminate myself in the
> hope that this, at least, would lead quickly to the scaffold.

Arrested in 1939 for the usual anti-government political
activities, Meyerhold was executed in Moscow in 1940.

While researching a BBC programme in 2005 on the writer
Isaac Babel, I stood before the altar of the St Catherine Nunnery
on which both Meyerhold and Babel had been tortured. I stood
and I wept, for the first time ruing the day that I had become a
communist. I stared, teary-eyed, at the electric leads that still
protruded from the stone floor. Above me, on the ceiling, someone had crudely scrawled over an icon to the Virgin Mary:

RELIGION IS THE OPIUM OF THE PEOPLE

The desecrator would have done well to study Marx's
quotation in full: 'Religion is the sigh of a suffering world, the
soul of a soul-less world. It's the drug that dulls the pain.
Religion is the opium of the people.'

After their torture Meyerhold and Babel, innocent men
both, had been carted off to the secret police headquarters,
the Lubyanka, where they were shot, cremated and had their
ashes taken to an unmarked grave in the cemetery adjoining
the Donskoi Monastery.

Perversely, Babel's ashes were interred along with those of
his tormentor, the secret police chief Nikolai Yezhov, executed
in February 1940. Isaac Babel had been one of the Soviet
Union's greatest writers, with such works as *Red Cavalry* and
Odessa Tales. However, he published virtually nothing in the
thirties and was accused of a menacing 'silence'. Once Stalin's

crimes were denounced in 1956, such authors as Isaac Babel, Boris Pilnyak and the poet Osip Mandelshtam were rehabilitated and published once again.

Those 'lucky' enough to avoid execution were packed into cattle trucks for week- or month-long journeys to labour camps in the permafrost of Siberia, the deserts of Kazakhstan or the Arctic Circle in Russia's Far North. If they survived the journey (many died of hypothermia or starvation en route), on arrival at the camps they mined coal or copper, dug for gold, sawed timber, built canals, power stations and whole towns. The cold and the poor food left the inmates constantly famished. The death rate was high and contingents of fresh prisoners were always available to replenish the labour force.

This was the fate awaiting Nikolai Starostin and the other footballers who had fallen foul of the regime – or were simply needed to make up the quotas. Nikolai was by no means unique in being a famous footballer brought low by the regime. On the other hand, as he said himself, to the extent that football is universal, the popular acclaim accorded to it by fans and even politicians may well have saved his life at a time when military and political leaders, poets, artists, engineers and scientists lost theirs. As he told me in one of our many conversations about his lost years:

'I naturally regret the "camp" years. Yet however strange it may seem, everywhere I went the football was always out of Beria's reach. Even though the notorious police chief had once been a player himself, he was never able to defeat me.'

Such was the power of football.

Starostin, the eldest of four footballing brothers, was born in 1902 in the village of Pogoist in Pskov province, some six hundred miles from Moscow. His father, a hunting guide, brought the family of six children (four boys, two girls) to Moscow where his employer, the Imperial Hunting Society, set the family up in a comfortable house in the district of Presnya, later to be called 'Red', or Krasnaya Presnya, for its part in the 1905 uprising. He died in the typhus epidemic of 1920 when Nikolai was eighteen; his brother Alexander was sixteen, Andrei was twelve and Pyotr was ten. To survive the famine years following the 1917 Revolution, the family sold the father's precious set of guns and paintings and Nikolai became the family provider. Being a talented football and ice hockey player, he made a living playing both sports according to season.

As a prominent sportsman, he inevitably came into contact with Alexander Kosarev, Secretary of the Young Communist League (Komsomol) and a member of the Communist Party's inner cabinet or Politburo. At that time, in the early 1930s, the Komsomol had considerable influence over sport. Indeed, the then Sports Minister, Ivan Kharchenko, was himself a former deputy Komsomol chief. Nikolai Starostin persuaded Kosarev to take up his idea of forming a new sports society separate from the two dominant nationwide clubs of Dinamo and the Red Army. The new society would cater for civilians, primarily those employed in cooperatives for garment-making, leatherwork, textiles and food. In search of a name, Nikolai recalled playing in 1927 against a German worker team called Spartacus, after the German communist Spartacus League which had been founded by Rosa Luxemburg and Karl Liebknecht and which had itself been named after the leader of the uprising of slaves in Rome in 73–71 BC.

Spartak was the first non-paramilitary society of its kind, set up in March 1935, and it quickly attracted top sportsmen and women. This was partly because the cooperatives were ploughing substantial funds into sport, but mainly because the society was run by the sportsmen and women themselves, free from the suffocating tutelage of the Secret-Service club, Dinamo, founded in 1923, and the armed forces Red Army Club, formed in 1928.

Initially, Spartak rented a sports ground in the Moscow suburbs originally equipped, in one of those ironies of history, by another four football-playing brothers – the Charnocks from Blackburn. The birth of Spartak heralded the start of a rivalry in Soviet and Russian sport that has lasted till today: Spartak versus Dinamo. Before 1936, the Dinamo teams (six in football's premier division alone) had held undisputed sway over football, as over most other sports. Spartak was now to challenge that supremacy.

It was that deadly rivalry that I unwittingly walked into in the summer of 1963. Not that I had any inkling then of the rivers of blood that had flowed because of it. It's a sobering thought that if I had played 25 years earlier I might also have received a bullet in the back of the head or found myself mining coal in an open-cast mine beyond the Arctic Circle.

In 1938, the new chief of the security forces, Lavrenty Beria, became honorary president of Dinamo. At the same time, Spartak had the political patronage of the Young Communist boss and friend of Starostin, Alexander Kosarev. The rivalry between the two sports societies and teams reflected the fight between the security forces and the Komsomol for control over Soviet sport. Dinamo had won the newly inaugurated football league in 1936, Spartak the new cup competition. In 1937, the positions were reversed. In the following two years, 1938–9, Spartak completed the 'golden double', a feat never repeated by any football team. The political repercussions of Dinamo's demise were about to make themselves felt throughout the sports movement. Football and other sports were already feeling the effects of arrests and persecution. Nikolai painstakingly took me through a list he'd written of those arrested. It contained hundreds of players and personal friends, even his brother-in-law Victor Prokofiev who'd also played for Spartak.

Nikolai and his friends knew full well that the 'repressed', as they were referred to, were impeccably honest and honourable people. But word had it that these players and officials had been abroad (albeit playing against communist worker teams) and, *ipso facto*, had been recruited by bourgeois agents as spies. Rumours of Spartak's involvement in illegal activities were rife. In fact, as Nikolai was later to admit, Spartak did pay higher wages than other clubs (payment being legal before the war), and he and his brothers were well remunerated for their success in league and cup. Their base salary was as high as 2,000 roubles (approximately £400) a month, compared to the average industrial worker's wage of 120 roubles. Nikolai admitted to me that he expected to be picked up by the police at any moment and for good reason: in the autumn of 1937 he and his brothers were denounced by the Soviet Union's most famous athletics stars, the brothers Serafim and Georgi Znamensky. Much later, in 2001, Georgi's daughter went on television to deny the official story of their deaths (that one had died heroically at the front, the other of his war wounds) and to reveal that her father and uncle had been secret police agents; Serafim had committed suicide.

The Znamensky brothers secretly accused Nikolai Starostin of trying to involve them in currency speculation, of buying expensive gifts for their wives when in Paris in July 1937 (playing a match against the communist team l'Etoile Rouge and visiting the Paris International Exhibition). They also said that

Nikolai had got army footballers discharged so that they could play for Spartak. This latter charge turned out to have some justification after it was revealed that a TsSKA goalkeeper, Vladislav Zhmelnikov, had left the forces two months early; for his pains he found himself playing for an army team in the remote Siberian town of Chita. Soon after, when war broke out, he was sent to the front and was later said to have turned to drink. Who could blame him?

For some reason, no action was taken then against the Starostin brothers. In a way they were lucky. Denunciations for such 'crimes' usually led to the death sentence. The communist authorities of the time encouraged denunciation as a patriotic duty: neighbour on neighbour, team-mate on team-mate, children on parents. Not only that: purge quotas were routinely drawn up for factory and farm, office and college, even sports clubs. Sometimes denunciations were a means of saving the skins of the denouncers.

The greatest shock for Starostin and Spartak members was the arrest in 1938 and subsequent execution of Kosarev, the club sponsor, now branded by the worst possible epithet, *vrag naroda*, 'enemy of the people'. 'Sasha', as he was familiarly known by Party leaders, had been the youngest-ever member of the Politburo; he was in his twenties and a genuine favourite with young people. He was an astute political operator and had always diligently supported Stalin's terror. How zealous he was became clear during the Politburo discussion of what sentence to give the 'right deviationist' Nikolai Bukharin, who had been arrested in May 1937 and whom Lenin had called 'the darling of the Party'. Nearly every Politburo member voted cautiously to back Stalin's decision, whatever it might be. Kosarev, however, demanded the death sentence.

That did not save him from the most horrific torture (to force him to confess to his 'treacherous' – and fictitious – crimes). He was finally executed (by a single shot in the back of the head) and, like many other eminent victims, taken at night to a burial ground and had his ashes scattered in an unknown grave. Rather strangely, while I was searching for the last resting place of the writer Isaac Babel's ashes (he was executed some time in 1940 or 1941), I came upon a small obelisk in the cemetery next to Moscow's Donskoi Monastery. It listed half a dozen political victims, including Kosarev. Although both Kosarev and Babel have since been rehabilitated, Babel's grave and the exact date of his execution have not been revealed to this day (nor have his confiscated twenty-one folders of unpublished work been returned to his family).

Kosarev was, in fact, the last of the first seven Komsomol leaders to be purged. Six were shot and one, Alexander Milchakov, spent fourteen years in a Siberian labour camp.

With Kosarev's arrest and that of others associated with Spartak, the Police Chief Beria was wreaking a terrible revenge on the sports society and other rivals to his beloved Dinamo club. Unlike his fellow political leaders and police chiefs, Beria was a fanatical football fan. In his youth he had even played at a fairly high level in his native Georgia and played in a match against a team led by Nikolai Starostin (which the Georgians lost). Starostin remembered him as a 'crude and dirty left-half'. When he became honorary president of Dinamo, Beria began to attend virtually every Moscow Dinamo home game. His fury was evident for all to see when the Dinamo team from the Georgian capital Tbilisi lost the 1939 Cup semi-final 1–0 to Spartak on a disputed goal. Not only was this an affront to Beria as a Georgian, it was a kick in the teeth for the secret police of which he was the all-powerful boss. The ubiquitous

Dinamo sports club existed alongside its patron, the security forces, in every major city. Beria evidently did not believe in fair play or in the inviolability of football results.

Since the referee, Ivan Gorelkin, was a former Dinamo player and a highly respected arbiter, the defeat was initially accepted and Spartak went on to win the final 3–1 against Leningrad Stalinets a fortnight later. To the astonishment of even the football authorities, however, a rematch was ordered from above (the NKVD – security forces) with Tbilisi Dinamo – even though the final was already over and done with. The original match referee, Gorelkin, was suspended (and shortly to be arrested) and it was almost impossible to find a replacement until the sports minister, Colonel Snegov, ordered the respected Nikolai Usov to officiate.

Spartak won a closely fought encounter 3–2 and, according to Starostin, 'When I glanced up at the VIP box, I saw Beria jump up, furiously kick over his chair and storm out of the stadium.'

Beria now sought a new way to suppress his team's rivals: he tried to have the Starostins arrested on many of the same charges that had surfaced in 1937. Nikolai suggested to me that they were saved by the Prime Minister, Molotov (after whom the infamous cocktail is named in the West), who refused to sign the arrest order. Nikolai put this 'stay of execution' down to the close friendship between his own daughter and that of Molotov. But the four Starostins and other Spartak players were ultimately to pay dearly for this affront to the NKVD and their deranged and terrifying boss, Lavrenty Beria.

Three years after Spartak's cup victory in 1939, Nikolai arrived home from training with the team, went to bed and was woken up in the middle of the night by a torch shining in his eyes and two pistols pointing at his head. It was 20 March 1942. He was arrested and hauled off to the Lubyanka in Moscow's city centre. He later discovered that his three brothers had been taken in, too, along with his two brothers-in-law, Pyotr Popov and Pavel Tikston, as well as his close friends and team-mates Yevgeny Arkhangelsk and Stanislav Leuta.

Nikolai was to spend the next eighteen months in the Lubyanka, mostly in solitary and constantly under interrogation. Initially he was charged with being involved in 'criminal activity led by enemy of the people Kosarev', who had already been executed. Specifically, he and his brothers were accused of plotting to assassinate Stalin and other leaders when they stood on the Mausoleum during the Red Square sports parade on May Day 1937. When that could not be substantiated – or when it was thought too risky to try to pin such a risible charge on the country's most popular footballers – Nikolai was accused of the much less serious crime of 'propagandizing bourgeois sport'. The charge read as follows: 'Nikolai Petrovich Starostin publicly praised bourgeois sport and tried to instil into our sport the mores of the capitalist world.'

The accusation was not simply that Starostin was running Spartak along bourgeois lines (with bonuses, transfers, tapping up other players, paying over the odds), but that he was using 'bourgeois' tactics and style of play that went against the collectivist principles of socialist football. Starostin was accused of encouraging individualist play and of allowing footballers to express themselves, thus resulting in a star system and hero-worship by the fans. Expressing yourself on a football pitch a crime!? Imagine the torture Pele would have undergone.

But that wasn't all. The prosecutor also charged that the four brothers had embezzled the considerable sum of 160,000 roubles from the club's sports goods shop, and that Nikolai had illegally obtained food and vodka for promising players who gained army exemption. No proof was advanced for the accusations. What was clear was the regime's, especially Beria's, anger at the popularity and independence of the brothers.

After prolonged 'interrogation', Nikolai finally owned up to making some criticism of Soviet sport and was 'persuaded' to think up anti-Soviet utterances he had heard from his brothers. That was the final basis of the charges against him and on which he was sentenced. While his interrogation had been harsh, it had not permanently disabled him. Pyotr, on the other hand, was left with tubercular lungs as a result of constant beatings and the damp conditions of his cell (well below ground level in the Lubyanka). Andrei was unable to walk for several months as a result of his treatment, being kept awake round the clock. What saved them from a worse fate at Beria's hands was, as Nikolai coined it, 'the place they held in the hearts of all football fans'. In the public's mind, he said, the Starostins personified Spartak. Beria was dealing not just with a few ordinary prisoners, but with the support and aspirations of millions of fans. In the short time of its existence, Spartak had swiftly become the most popular Soviet team.

In November 1943, the four brothers were brought before the Supreme Court Military Tribunal (that same tribunal which already had sentenced thousands to death). The charges were read out and the accused were asked for their pleas. They each in turn admitted to making the cited comments, without realizing they constituted a criminal offence. Within three days the court delivered its sentence.

Nikolai, Andrei and Alexander were found guilty of 'lauding bourgeois sport and endeavouring to drag bourgeois mores into the Soviet system of physical culture' whereas Pyotr was charged with having been overheard to say that 'the collective farms were not justifying themselves and that Soviet engineers were not paid enough'. However ridiculous the charges might sound today, in the hysteria of the time, especially it being wartime, they were considered almost treasonable.

As members of the Communist Party, each brother was sentenced to ten years' hard labour. The non-Party members among the accused got eight years. The moments before being driven away from court were the last they would share together for twelve long years. All the same, as Nikolai later remarked to me with classic Russian understatement, 'ten years hard labour was a virtual "Not Guilty" verdict for the time. The future seemed not so gloomy after all.'

There now began for Nikolai an extraordinary, if harsh, life in far-flung camps – first in the Ukhta oilfield within the Arctic Circle for a year, then in the Soviet Far East, initially at Khabarovsk on the Amur River, then at Komsomolsk-on-Amur. Wherever he went he found camp commandants vying for his services as football coach. As irony would have it, he was now much sought after as coach to the local Dinamo teams, inasmuch as all the camps came under the jurisdiction of the security forces.

As a result, Nikolai Starostin had extensive privileges – to live outside the camps, sharing with the other players in digs close to the local stadium, to exist 'more like an exile than a political prisoner' – a far cry from the fate of the non-footballing fraternity, like Boris Pasternak's Lara in *Doctor Zhivago*, or Osip Mandelshtam, or the Spanish and German communists seeking refuge from Franco and Hitler in the 'fraternal' Soviet Union, or the engineers, priests and yeoman (*kulak*) farmers. Nikolai himself tried to explain how football was unique in this respect because people seemed to separate it from all that was going on around them, especially the arrests, imprisonment, exile and execution of millions of Soviet citizens. Starostin likened it to the worship by sinners desperately seeking oblivion in their appeal to a divinity. For most people football was the only, and sometimes the last, chance and hope of retaining a tiny island of sincere feelings and human dignity.

With guards and criminals alike, Starostin became a hero. No one was permitted to lay a hand on him. As he once told me, back in the safety of his Moscow flat, 'even inveterate recidivists would sit as quiet as mice to listen to my football stories'.

One small consolation for the Starostins, as for other political prisoners, was that they were spared the horrors of the Second World War. Indeed, one sports bureaucrat and Russian Olympic Committee member, Vladimir Rodichenko, once tried to convince me that the regime had deliberately sent the Starostins to Siberia to save them from the war (what he did not explain was why they were kept in exile until well after the war). The end of hostilities in May 1945 found Nikolai Starostin still coaching Dinamo teams a third of the way round the world from Russia's war-ravaged western borders.

It was in the post-war atmosphere of purges and Great Russian chauvinism after a great military victory over fascism that Nikolai Starostin's life was to take another incredible turn. In the middle of the night, sometime in 1948, he was woken up by the local Party Secretary in his Siberian outpost with urgent news: 'Stalin is on the phone. Quick!' Half an hour later, Nikolai picked up the receiver and heard the voice of, not the dictator, but his elder son, Vasily.

Nikolai had come to know Vasily back in the late 1930s when Nikolai's daughter, Yevgenia, had been a member of the Spartak horse-riding club. She had made friends with a 'skinny, unremarkable lad by the name of Volkov.' As Nikolai Starostin was the Spartak general manager, he was privy to the information that Volkov's real name was Vasily Stalin. During the war, Vasily was to become the world's youngest general at eighteen and the commander-in-chief of the Soviet air force. Now Vasily was sending his personal aircraft to bring Nikolai back to Moscow where he was to become chief coach to the air force football team, Krylya Sovetov, 'Wings of the Soviets'.

Life, of course, was not so simple. As Nikolai said of the time, 'man proposes and God disposes'. He knew well that implacable hatred existed between Vasily Stalin and the police chief Beria. Not surprisingly, therefore, Beria's police spies soon tracked Nikolai down and gave him twenty-four hours to quit the capital. Once again Nikolai found himself an exile, this time in the Kazakhstan capital, Alma-Ata, where he was recruited to train the local team, Kairat – whose centre-forward was to give me the run-around in my second Spartak game.

Soon after Stalin's death in March 1953, Beria was arrested and shot by the new leadership. 'It was like the sun rising in the Far North after the long polar night,' Starostin was to tell me later. 'Surprise, joy and hope were all mixed together. A month later I heard my wife's excited voice telling me that my sentence was being reviewed.' It was time to thank Spartak's rival, Dinamo. As he wrote in his memoirs about himself and his brothers, 'Our family must express its gratitude to Dinamo. In those terrible years it was the island on which we survived, keeping our families together and finally enabling me to return to Moscow.'

It was only with Nikolai's autobiography, published in 1989, that the whole truth could be told. He eagerly presented me with a copy, asking that I do my best to have it translated and published in as many countries as possible. Andrei, it turns out, had ended up with his brother-in-law Tikston in the dreaded Norilsk camp, mining copper in north-eastern Siberia. There they came upon the only woman sports minister in Soviet times, E. L. Knopova, purged after only three months in office, even though 'she had done all she could to persecute the Starostin family', as Nikolai put it. Just desserts perhaps. Andrei also met Alexander Kosarev's wife and daughter in the Norilsk camp, both of them sentenced to ten years. It was common for the immediate relatives of 'repressed' victims to be judged 'guilty by association' and incarcerated.

As for the other two brothers, Pyotr first worked at an iron and steel plant, then became an engineer at a hydro-electric station and, subsequently, manager of a cement works. Alexander had the worst time of it, toiling at a lumber camp in the Siberian *taiga*.

All four now had their Communist Party membership restored upon their return to Moscow, and their sentences were declared invalid. Alexander and Andrei returned as football coaches, while Nikolai, now aged fifty, took charge of Spartak as general manager, a post he had held in 1936, and now returned to in 1955. He worked at his job in both a full-time and honorary capacity up to his death. He survived his two younger brothers, Alexander and Andrei, both of whom died of heart attacks in their early eighties. Pyotr was still hale and hearty when I met him in 1992, but he did not outlive his eldest brother, dying a year earlier, in 1995.

The last time I met Nikolai was a year before his death in 1996. He was as gaunt and short-sighted as ever, and his joints were beginning to creak – though he did not use a walking stick. Full of life and optimism, he remained true to his beloved Spartak. Despite his terrible treatment at the hands of the regime, he insisted that he remained a communist in his heart and was clearly out of place in the new oligarch-dominated Russian society, despising the 'drunken clown' of a President, Boris Yeltsin. He was extremely proud of his three Orders of Lenin – the Soviet Union's supreme award (no other Russian sports person had received such honours). After his death, a statue was erected to him close to Spartak's home ground, the Lenin Stadium.

What a man. What a life. Nikolai lived modestly on his pension in a two-roomed flat, did his own cooking and cleaning, and still made occasional trips to watch the club he'd created and served for nigh on sixty years. If Nikolai had any regrets, apart from the irretrievably lost years in the camps, it was that the footballers of today did not possess the broad cultural and vital outlook of the players of his time. As he told me the last time I saw him, 'It always astounds me that today's players seem to have no interests beyond video and rock cassettes. I believe fervently that you cannot separate culture from football; football cognoscenti should be cognoscenti of literature and the arts as well.'

Many footballers would not understand that. The incomparably greater freedom to live and play in Russia, and elsewhere, has today resulted in narrower specialization and almost complete lack of culture in modern footballers. I once mentioned Starostin's words to Alexei Smertin. Being a devotee of the English novelist John Fowles (whom we visited together at his home in Lyme Regis in 2005 – Fowles was as much in awe of Smertin as the footballer was of him, and kept a picture of Alexei on his mantelpiece), he agreed entirely, saying how sad it was that his then Chelsea team-mates never read a book, and only looked at pictures in the tabloids during their journeys to football grounds.

All the same, today's freedom in Russia has enabled Nikolai Starostin's amazing story to be told. It offers a glimpse into the Soviet Union's darkest years and sheds light on one of the most dreadful episodes which footballers and sportsmen and women had endured anywhere in the world.

Yet Starostin's story also demonstrates something else: the immense power and vitality of football, its ability not only to engage the popular consciousness, but to restrain the arbitrary actions of brutal tyrants.

12

GOING HOME

After five years in Moscow it was now decision-time. Spartak had dispensed with my services and translating did not exactly inspire creative endeavour. I was keen to complete my doctoral dissertation on Soviet sport at Birmingham University and start writing my own books. Not only that. I was keen to undertake missionary work within the Communist Party and attempt to alter dogmatic views about the Soviet system. There were still many British comrades clinging to an idealized vision of what was going on in a land they'd never visited (or if they had, they'd had their prejudices confirmed by seeing only what they wanted to see). As someone privileged enough to have seen the Soviet Union from the inside for five years, I felt I was in a good position to set the record straight.

Annick and I had another reason for going home. I now had two daughters, Tania and Nadine, who were yet to see their parents' countries of birth or meet their relatives. Also, my confidence in Soviet schooling had been on the wane since those limited and limiting classes at the HPS, and I wanted the girls to enjoy the best schooling available to them.

We had never planned to settle permanently in Russia, and wanted the girls to be educated in the English system. My departure, however, was not all plain sailing. I was helped on my way by the boot of the Party whose international representative (our old friend Molchanov who'd reported our 'reformist tendencies' at the Higher Party School in 1961–2) took exception to an article I'd written for the British-Soviet Friendship journal. What particularly bugged him was the title: 'The Growing Pains of Soviet Youth' (which the editor, not me, had chosen).

I was called in for questioning at Friendship House, a relatively neutral venue. No doubt someone of my standing didn't merit an office at Molchanov's place of work, the vast white building near the Kremlin that housed the Party Central Committee. At the carbuncle-encrusted palace on Kropotkin Street, not far from the city centre, I was ushered into a marble and malachite-decorated room to await my 'interrogation'. I can't say I was nervous or fearful, more bemused. How on earth had some official found fault with an article that heaped praise on the achievements of Soviet youth? It did not cross my mind that some fifteen years before, while Stalin was still alive, suspects had been summoned, just like me, arrested, judged and shot. For saying too much. For saying too little. For saying nothing at all. Some had suffered in error, for the wrong interpretation of their words. Surely this couldn't happen to me? Stalin was dead and buried along with the sinister 'ism' he had inspired.

In came Molchanov, looking grim (nothing new there) and quite hostile. He sat down at the other side of the table and, without a greeting or small talk, asked me a direct question.

'Comrade Riordan, would you say Soviet society is socialist?'

What's this? One of those quiz shows where you mustn't say 'yes' or 'no' or hesitate? Well, if he wanted a straight answer, fine.

'Er, yes, more or less.'

He ignored the hedging. Second question.

'Is socialism a progressive stage of social development?'

Was he testing me on what I'd learned at the Higher Party School? Marx had made it plain that socialism was a higher and more progressive stage of development than capitalism.

'Certainly.'

Now came the clincher that told me right away what this was all about.

'Then, tell me, if you please, how pains can grow worse as socialism develops.'

So that was it. My article entitled 'The Growing Pains of Soviet Youth'. I didn't bother explaining that the editor, Pat Sloan, had softened my 'Problems of Soviet Youth' to 'Growing Pains'. I tried explaining that in English 'growing pains' did not mean that problems multiply, but that young people experience temporary pains as they grow up.

Hence the analogy. It did no good. Perhaps the nuances of English were too much for him or perhaps he didn't want to go back on his translation for the Central Committee. Either way, after debating other infelicities, he lost his temper and branded me an *anti-sovetchik*. Now that was fighting talk: in Stalin's time people were shot with precisely that label round their necks.

This was plainly ridiculous. I'd written an article for a magazine with a readership of one man and his dog (the government might have bought thousands, for all I knew, to defray costs), and my title (or, rather, the editor's title) had been mistranslated. For that I was 'anti-Soviet'? It reminded me of poor Tom Botting being sent to Siberia for something he *didn't* say on Moscow Radio. This time it was me in the firing line, the victim of unreason for which there was plainly no defence. In capitalist Britain at least there were support agencies to turn to: civil rights lawyers, the law courts, the media, witnesses for the defence, friends and colleagues. Here I had no one. The serious *anti-sovetchik* accusation made me aware of my utter impotence in a society that lacked the essential safeguards of any democracy: checks and balances. Where were those checks and balances for someone accused of 'treachery' by the Central Committee of the Communist Party of the Soviet Union? How could I defend myself?

Fortunately, I'd already made it clear at my workplace that I was leaving. So the Central Committee left the matter there. Or so I thought. Once back in Britain, however, I found that all requests for an entry visa to Russia were rejected. I was barred from re-entry.

Although I'd handed in my notice at Progress Publishers weeks before, my farewell visit was nothing short of extraordinary. The chief editor, trade union chief and a couple of control editors I passed in the corridor shunned me as if I was a pariah; worse, a non-person. I didn't exist. Someone repeated the *anti-sovetchik* epithet under the breath as I walked by, making it clear who had put the mockers on me. A wave of sadness overcame me. I had worked cheek by jowl with these people for three years; we'd feasted and clinked glasses together (consumed a pood of salt, as the Russian saying goes) and I hoped that we considered one another firm friends. Yet, now, all at once, they were turning their backs on me, on the say-so of a Party hack who'd stuck a label on me – like the yellow Star of David under the Nazis.

Not for the first time I told myself I'd never understand the Russians. But, then again, perhaps I ought to be more understanding of a people who in a single lifetime had undergone so many traumas: revolution, civil war, collectivization, helter-skelter industrialization, the Great Terror and a devastating world war. Enough to make people play safe, keep their heads down, at least pay lip service to the current Kremlin line. Outsiders like me could be sacrificed.

I departed under a cloud, unable to clear my name. No one had read the offending article; they accepted my damnation from on high – just as the Writers' Union had once done with Boris Pasternak without reading his 'heretical' novel *Doctor Zhivago*. Most of them had never read it. Zealots of any sort, whether political or religious, have one thing in common: intolerance based on ignorance.

For the next five years, 1965–70, I was to be denied a re-entry visa. Chance alone came to my rescue. Out of the blue, while unemployed, I received a phone call one day from a specialist travel agency, asking if I could lead a tourist party to Moscow the following week. They'd lost their leader at the last moment and had been put on to me as someone who spoke Russian and was acquainted with Moscow. I agreed at once and was recruited with a fast-track visa that may have evaded security clearance.

On my return to Moscow, I visited my old next-door neighbour, who doubled as KGB chief as well as personnel officer at Progress Publishers. Our families had got on well and he now fixed things for me to receive a visa for future visits. However abhorrent to me this was, I was playing the game according to Soviet rules – exploiting personal friendships rather than going through the due process (*what due process?*) to clear my name of the black mark I hadn't merited.

Henceforth I was able to make yearly trips to Moscow where I could watch my old club Spartak. Like Pompey, they had fallen on hard times.

After being runners-up in the season I played for them, 1963, Spartak fell to eighth (of 16 clubs) in both the 1964 and 1965 seasons, with as many defeats as victories. By 1966, they had improved to fourth, yet then fell back to seventh in 1967. In 1969, however, Simonyan again assembled a winning squad which broke the three-year monopoly of Dinamo Kiev as league champions. My old pals Logofet and Khusainov were still playing, but Igor Netto had hung up his boots. The team had been strengthened by the experienced Georgian goalkeeper Anzor Kavazashvili and three youthful players, Abramov, Lovchev and Kalinov. That season, the team won the league title, suffering only two defeats, scoring 51 goals to 15 against. Spartak was not to repeat that success for another decade. Portsmouth, meanwhile, had dropped like a stone from the top of Division 1 to the bottom of Division 4.

Once home, none of the stupid charade in Moscow prevented me from campaigning within the British Communist Party for a different line on Soviet communism. Much to the annoyance of my seniors, I would not keep my mouth shut. I pointed out that we needed to tell the truth about the Soviet Union, rather than constantly having to defend the indefensible and regurgitating their now lazy propaganda. We needed an objective analysis of real-live communism as it existed in the USSR, Eastern Europe, China and Cuba. Otherwise, why should anyone respect or believe us? In a paper I privately circulated among left-wing friends in 1971, I highlighted three main issues.

1. The idea that the socialism in the USSR and other 'socialist' states had changed out of all recognition from the original ideals of the October Revolution.

2. The Soviet Union and those that followed were one-party states whose communist parties never offered themselves in free elections or permitted dissenting views in any area of human endeavour, be it literature, art, history or even sport.

3. Stalin's dictatorship and the purges needed to be examined. How had this come about? How had the ideals of Marx and Engels or the founders of the Soviet state been lost? What lessons should we draw for socialism in Britain?

Generally speaking, I was spitting into the wind. For Party strategists and the old guard, I was a heretic trying to ruin fraternal relations. As some critics in my Party branch put it, seeking an old and trusted badge of shame, I was a 'Trotskyist'. Undaunted, I helped set up a specialist study group involving a dozen intellectuals with an interest in Eastern Europe. The Party gave us its seal of approval – *as long as we did not publish anything*. We met, invited non-Party experts on the left (a most unusual break with communist tradition), debated issues and sent our concerted views to the Party leadership. As far as I know, they fell on deaf ears.

Soon after my return in late 1965, my Party branch voted to expel me for 'bourgeois bohemianism' (I never did discover what on earth that meant) because of my 'anti-Soviet' views. With six abstentions, two for the motion and three against, I survived by the skin of my teeth. The qualities of a good centre-half, solidity and stubbornness, counted for something. Frankly, if they had not tried to expel me, I would probably have told them where to stuff my Party card. Now I was even more determined to prove them wrong. Then a series of events occurred that swung things my way. In the spring of 1968 communist reformists in Czechoslovakia led by my old Moscow Party School pal Alexander Dubček announced that they intended to 'build socialism with a human face'. For a start, they declared that no communist party had the right to govern without free elections. Otherwise, what does democracy mean? The astute and compassionate Dubček was only too aware that after dictatorship and political repression in the Soviet Union and China, communism was synonymous in many people's minds with the very negation of democracy.

I was delighted. This was what *I* was agitating for. Now surely we could make progress and my comrades would see the light. But, sadly, it was a false dawn. Soviet tanks crushed the 'Prague Spring' and arrested the new Czechoslovak communist leaders, expelling them, including Dubček, from the Party. It was a sign of the new times that, unlike the Hungarian Party rebel Imre Nagy, Dubček was not executed. Instead, he was given a minor forestry post in far-off Bohemia. After the fall of the communist regime in 1989, he was elected speaker of the National Assembly in Prague but sadly died in a car crash in 1992. The world was a lesser place without him. The events of the Prague Spring proved once and for all the impossibility of any potential democratic communist state under the Soviet system. Through their ruthlessness, fear and bigotry the Soviet leaders themselves crushed the last chance for communism in Europe.

After the Prague Spring, the British Communist Party, like other Western European counterparts, split asunder as members had to face up to where their loyalties lay: to the

Soviet Union or to their own country, building socialism by violence and revolution, or by national traditions of parliamentary democracy. The majority followed the Party leadership which tried tentatively to distance itself from Moscow. This new line was described as 'Eurocommunism' or 'polycentrism' – a many-centred organization rather than everything revolving around Moscow. It was too little, too late. Membership of communist parties dwindled rapidly as leaders and members argued over the correct road to socialism and, particularly, the line to take with the Soviet Union.

I never did leave the Communist Party, it left me. In November 1991, by 135 votes to 72, the last Party congress disbanded the Party which had been my spiritual home for thirty-two years, and had given me the opportunity to study at the Higher Party School and see Soviet life at first-hand. Its successor, Democratic Left, intended to make 'a rupture with past undemocratic practices . . . a break from the disastrous Soviet mould'.

However, all the new organization aspired to be was a focus for discussion that could lead to joint initiatives and campaigns. It was doomed from the start. Like the one-time deputy editor of the *Daily Worker*, George Matthews, I joined Democratic Left, dutifully, even though privately I was lukewarm about its wishy-washy agenda. I agreed with George that 'there are some things I wish I'd never done and I do regret. [But I'm] sorry it had to end as it did.'

Away from political struggles, I had landed on my feet on returning to England in 1965. I gained a string of university posts, ending up as lecturer in Russian Studies in 1971 at Bradford University where I remained for the next eighteen years, climbing the ladder to professor. I never hid my politics. Generally speaking, reds have been able to make it in some

British institutions, by no means all – like the armed forces, the judiciary, civil service and public corporations like the BBC.

I may have been lucky to find university work on my return from Moscow but my marriage did not survive the transition. Living together in the normality of England exposed cracks that living apart in Moscow and Picardy had papered over. After a few acrimonious months, we resolved to call it a day on the grounds, as the divorce papers state, of 'incompatibility', which was an understatement. As with many 'incompatible' couples, the people who really suffered, from both constant bickering and the eventual split, were the children. Tania and Nadine remained with their mother, as is the British custom, and I moved in with my mother in Portsmouth.

After my divorce from Annick I took up with a Soviet Tatar who had married my fellow translator Jeff Vegoda in Moscow. Jeff lived in London with his elderly Jewish mother whom he'd hoped to persuade to accept his new (non-Jewish, with Muslim name, Rashida) wife. She wouldn't. In the end, Jeff chose to stay loyal to his mother and asked me to find accommodation and employment for Rashida. We drifted together, married after her divorce from Jeff and had three children: Sean, Nathalie and Catherine (aka Salavat, Onara and Gulnara, as their Tatar names). After some twenty-five years together we parted and I now live alone with my cat, Tilly. My old Yorkshire tom, Pompey, survived long enough to help Portsmouth climb back up to Division 2, the Championship – I never left for a match without stroking him three times and intoning 'Help Pompey win!' Sadly, he did not live beyond 17 to see the glories of the Premiership under Harry Redknapp.

While I moved up the ladder professionally, my football club, Portsmouth, were sliding to the bottom: from top of the football league in 1950 to bottom of Division 4 by the mid-1970s. By the time I moved to Bradford they were struggling to survive. For me the only good to come out of it was a regular excursion every other Saturday to famous old clubs now wallowing in the football mire. From twelve clubs that had founded the Football League at Manchester's Royal Hotel on 17 April 1888, the League had expanded to ninety-two clubs a hundred years later. Many were in the north, within an hour or so by car from Bradford. My son and I would follow Pompey westwards to Burnley, Bury, Preston, Rochdale, Wigan, Oldham, Blackburn, Stockport, Tranmere and even Wrexham, eastwards to Hull, Grimsby, Hartlepool and Scarborough, up to York, Darlington and Scunthorpe, and south to Halifax, Huddersfield, Barnsley, Rotherham, Sheffield Wednesday, Doncaster Rovers and Notts County.

A different sort of football from Spartak: meat pies and polystyrene cups of Bovril, antiquated urinals and unmown grass. Money for modernizing the less fashionable northern football grounds was hard to come by. Several would not have met the safety regulations established for teams in the higher reaches of the Football League. It was a disaster waiting to happen. And it struck on the final day of the 1984–5 season, 11 May. It is as fresh in my memory as if it were yesterday, and the tears start even now when I think back on it.

That particular season was one the Queen might have called an *annus horribilis*. It saw some of the worst fan violence in English history. Hooligan gangs appeared to be trying to outdo each other in creating the greatest mayhem. Trouble flared at both legs of the Milk Cup semi-final, between Sunderland and Chelsea and, then, at Luton's Kenilworth Road on 13 March in the match between the home side, Luton, and Millwall. Following the game, there was a horrific pitched battle between Millwall fans and the police.

Seats were torn out, innocent fans terrorized, missiles flung. At one point, a policeman who was attempting to give the kiss of life to an unconscious colleague was kicked and beaten by two youths. Altogether, forty-seven people were injured, most of them policemen. Marauding Millwall fans left a trail of destruction through the town which led, via a wrecked train, all the way back to the East End of London.

This was no isolated incident: it all came as part of a cycle of mounting violence and racist abuse of black footballers. Two weeks later, the Prime Minister, Margaret Thatcher, called a Cabinet meeting to demand that football clubs and the game's governing body curb the menace. There were many anticipating the end of the season when clubs could look forward to a fresh start after the summer break with no substantial changes made. But fate intervened.

A tragedy occurred at Bradford's Valley Parade stadium. On that final day, Saturday 11 May, I can only say what many fans throughout the country must have uttered with a deep sigh: there but for the grace of God go I. It could have happened to any of us, at any of the old grounds. I was lucky. Instead of going to Valley Parade on that sunny afternoon, I drove with my son and brother to Huddersfield for the Second Division game with Pompey before 13,000 spectators. Kevin O'Callaghan and Vince Hilaire ('He's here, he's there, he's every-f . . . . . . -where, Vince Hilaire!') scored in Pompey's 2–0 win. It wasn't enough to ensure promotion, however; that went to Manchester City on goal difference.

Our happy mood at getting the win was shattered on our return to Bradford where we heard the terrible news. Five minutes before half-time in the Third Division game between Bradford and Lincoln City someone in the seventy-seven-year-old main stand dropped a cigarette end. It slipped through the wooden floorboards and fell among tinder-dry litter that had been allowed to gather, untouched, for years. In next to no time the whole stand was alight. At first, smoke and small flames appeared in the top right corner. Then, slowly and inexorably, the fire spread until it became an inferno. So hot was it that it set light to people sixty yards away; a policeman on the pitch near the halfway line suddenly burst into flames (and later died in Bradford Infirmary).

Next afternoon, the *Look North* TV programme showed the entire horrific course of the fire. I sat in the safety of my own home, appalled and in tears.

Fifty-six people died, many of them packed in front of the locked gates behind the burning stand. Everyone in Bradford seemed to know someone who had perished. A disabled friend of my eighteen-year-old son had been in the wheelchair enclosure at the front of the main stand – he and others stood no chance. Ironically, the match was to celebrate Bradford's promotion to the Second Division. A year later and the stadium would have come under the provisions of the Safety of Sports Grounds Act.

The Bradford fire, alongside the Heysel tragedy which took place just eighteen days later, changed the course of English football. The FA banned all League clubs from competing in Europe for a year. UEFA extended the ban indefinitely, and FIFA applied the ban to the rest of the world. Parliament forbade the sale of alcohol at football grounds. Crucially, the Taylor Report that followed the Bradford fire resulted in all-seater grounds.

These days I sit in relative comfort at Fratton Park, out of the rain, alongside my eldest daughter Tania, granddaughter Marie, grandson Perry and son Sean. My youngest daughter takes her seat at Elland Road, cheering on Leeds, and my son-in-law does the same at Nottingham Forest. It's all a far cry from my boyhood, being passed over heads down the packed terraces to the perimeter wall, perching atop a metal bar, with the smells of beer and Woodbines, the sound of rattles and good-natured banter (no swearing in those days). How football has changed: TV coverage, all-seater stadiums, Big Business, Russian oligarchs, and multi-billionaire crooks. Yet, one thing has survived: the sheer joy of the game. Nothing and no one can destroy that.

Some Sunday mornings I sit over coffee and croissants with my pal, ex-Russian captain Alexei Smertin (he holds the record: four croissants at one sitting – yet he is as skinny as a goalpost). We talk about football today and reminisce about yesterday. I tell him how, in Soviet times, the major grounds were packed to capacity, whereas today the six main Moscow teams – Spartak, TsSKA, Dinamo, Lokomotiv, Torpedo and the newly formed Moskva – average a mere 7,000 fans a game. He explains that there is a lack of interest in the domestic game now that non-Russian republics have split off and that top players like himself can travel the football world.

I put it to him how murder and corruption now dominate Russian football – match-fixing, bribery and intimidation of referees – and big business and politics – hit killings of oligarch rivals and journalists (more than 5,000 such killings took place in 2006 alone. Many were oppositionists, like the journalists Anna Politkovskaya, in Moscow, and Alexander Litvinenko, in London). Alexei admits that corruption exists – which is why he opts to play in England – but he insists that the Russian President is trying to put things right. 'It's transition,' he says. 'Give us time. Russia needs time.'

He is right. Change cannot come overnight. But when I talk of the past he often switches off, as if the past is a foreign country, a painful memory to forget.

That brings me back to conversations with my old Spartak team-mates who had 'lost their memory'. Worse still, when I returned to Moscow in 2007 for a BBC programme on the Higher Party School, *no one* would talk to me. Tania, the Komsomol friend after whom we had named our first daughter – 'too busy, urgent work'. Vitaly Kostomarov, our Russian teacher, suddenly vanished after sounding pleased to hear me over the telephone. The old rector who failed to turn up to an arranged meeting . . .

Not for the first time I realized that in Russia memory of history is overlaid with complexities. Some individuals are unable to reflect on their lives because they have grown accustomed to avoiding awkward questions about anything, not least their own moral choices at defining moments in their lives. Others are reluctant to admit to actions of which they are ashamed, often justifying their behaviour by citing motives and beliefs that were imposed upon their pasts.

After such a radical break with Soviet communism, switching to Yeltsin's 'robber baron' mayhem and Putin's state capitalism, it is perhaps hardly surprising that many choose to block out the past and find solace in the medieval ritual of the Russian Orthodox Church rather than the football stadium. As the tragic poet Anna Akhmatova put it:

> *As if I were a river*
> *The harsh age changed my course,*
> *Replaced one life with another,*
> *Flowing in a different channel*
> *And I do not recognize my shores.*

Back in the late 1980s, under Gorbachov, when the crimes of Stalin were being uncovered, there was a popular saying: 'A nation that does not know its past has no future.'

Memory is more important for Russians today than it ever was. But, then, hadn't two of my surviving comrades at the Higher Party School also refused to talk in the past?

I am lucky. For me memory is something to treasure. In facing up to the brevity of my future I take pleasure in the great hinterland of memory and experience that I can visit. I don't bask in eternal euphoric sunshine – how could I when Pompey regularly let me down and I dwell on errors of my past? But between dark days I have experienced wonderful moments of joy and insight as well as much happiness. I am content.

There is, of course, one memory that stands above all others: running out to the familiar jingle and the rush of the crowd's roar in Moscow's Lenin Stadium with the No. 5 on my back. Nothing can better that.

ACKИOЩLEDGEMEИTS

With thanks to my London comrade, Steve, for his diaries on our time in Moscow; they were invaluable in putting the record straight. And to my three editors, Richard Collins, Jack Fogg and Robin Harvie, much gratitude for all your hard work.

INDEX

JR denotes Jim Riordan.

A History of Twentieth-Century Russia (Service) 179
Akhmadulina, Bella 178
Akhmatova, Anna 211
Albert Road Junior School, Southsea 28
Ambartsumyan, Slava 143
Anderson, Jock 20
Ararat FC 147
Arkhangelsk, Yevgeny 189
Armenia 112–13, 147
Arsenal FC 25–6
Attlee, Clement 22–3, 49
Auden, W. H. 162
Azerbaidzhan 113–14

Babel, Isaac 181–2, 187
Bacuzzi, Joe 24, 25
Barker, Geoff 48, 49
Barstow, Stan 52
Baykov, Alexander 48, 49
BBC 48, 52, 145, 150, 153, 163, 181, 211
Beckett, Francis 80
Bedny, Demyan 51
Beeching, Bill 86
Beeching, Elsie 86
Bell, Julian 162
Bennett, Alan 38

Beria, Lavrenty 23, 60, 72, 74, 182, 184, 187, 190, 193
Berlin, Germany 41, 42, 43–5
Bernal, J. D. 162
Beskov, Konstantin 121
Best, George 153
Birmingham University 47, 48–51, 56, 127, 197
Blackburn Rovers 93
Blake, George 173
Blunt, Anthony 74, 161–3
Bobrov, Vsevolod 24, 25, 121
Bolshoi Theatre 118
Botting, Tom 99–100, 104, 200
Bradford FC 208–9
Bradford University 205–6
Braine, John 52
Breslin, George 99, 104
Brezhnev, Leonid 70–1, 118, 139
British Ally 158, 166
British Army on the Rhine (BAOR) 45–6, 131
British Consular Club (Moscow) 90–1, 126, 129, 132
British Diplomatic Corps (Moscow) 90–1, 126, 129, 132, 133
British Foreign Office 105, 163, 164

British-Soviet Friendship Society (BSFS) 55–6, 91–2, 120, 198
Bromley, D. B. 5–6
Brown, Jennifer (step-sister) 27
Brown, Marilyn (step-sister) 17, 27
Brown, Ron (step-father) 16, 17, 21–2
Brown, Terry (step-brother) 27
Bruckner, Wilbur M. 164
Buck, Tim 70
Bukharin, Nikolai 186
Bull, Roy 60, 117
Burgess, Guy 1, 74, 91, 120, 156, 157, 158, 160, 161–5, 166–70, 173, 174
Burman, Mark 153
Butler, Ernie 21

Cambridge University 38, 48, 74, 156, 158, 160, 161, 162–3, 175
Campaign for Nuclear Disarmament (CND) 52
Camus, Albert 6
Carre, John le 163
Carter, Raich 22
Castro, Fidel 86, 118
Central Army Sports Club, TsSKA 46, 88, 131, 186, 210
Chamberlain, Neville 11
Charnock, Harry 93, 184
Charnock, Robert 93–4, 184
Charnock, Willy 93, 184
Chekhov, Anatoly 114–15
Chelsea 24–5, 86, 196
Chernova, Tania 115
Chilston, Viscount 105
Chukovsky, Kornei 116, 118
Churchill, Winston 22, 113, 122, 124
CIA 53, 163, 164
Clarke, Ike 21
Cohen, Gabriel 101

Cohen, Rose 99, 104, 105
Cold War 3, 4, 26, 38, 43, 156
Comintern 64, 75, 97–8, 101
Communism:
    effect of 20th CPSU Congress and Hungarian uprising upon worldwide image of 49, 53, 54, 70, 81, 99, 157, 174–5
    end of European 154, 204–5
    JR's sympathies towards see Riordan, James William
    sport and 77–8, 127–9, 183, 184
    spread of 4–5, 77
Communist Party of Great Britain (CPGB) 1, 4, 23, 42, 55, 60, 116–17
    Cambridge cell 162
    Comintern Congress with 1920 97–8
    direct subsidy from Moscow 80–1
    drop in membership 1957 53–4, 175
    Eurocommunism 205
    headquarters 57
    Higher Party School and 69–70, 71, 81
    intellectuals 74, 162
    JR joins 54
    JR protests against dogmatic view of Soviet Union 197, 202–5
    officials in Moscow 61, 69, 97–106
    persecution of members in Soviet Union 97–106
    'polycentrism' 205
    relationship between Soviet Communist Party and 5, 61, 69–75, 80–1, 97–106, 118
    split due to Prague spring 204–5
    Stalin's crimes and 53, 97–106

Communist Party of the Soviet
   Union (CPSU)
   Central Committee 72–3, 74, 83,
      107, 123, 169, 198, 200
   perks for prominent members of
      83–4, 123–4
   relationship between CPGB and
      5, 61, 69–75, 80–1, 97–106, 118
   17th Party Congress 179–80
   20th Party Congress 49, 53, 54, 70,
      81, 99, 157, 174–5
   21st Party Congress 68
Communist Party of the United
   States 67–8
Cornforth, Maurice 162, 163
Cuba 86, 118
Cuban Missile Crisis 3, 137
Czechoslovakia 174, 204

Daily Express 104
Daily Mail 156, 172
Daily Mirror 46, 47
Daily Sketch 25
Daily Worker 23, 24, 53, 54–5, 72,
      81, 98, 106, 118, 157, 158, 166,
      173, 205
Dalglish, Robert 101, 158
Darwin, Charles 162
Davies, Bob 48, 49
Day-Lewis, Cecil 162
Delapenha, Lindy 12
Dementiev, Nikolai 131
Democratic Left 205
Denyer, Stu 31
Dexter, Tom 101
Dickinson, Jimmy 20, 21, 87
Dinamo Kiev 202
Dixon, Richard 123–4, 158
Dobb, Maurice 162
Doctor Zhivago (Pasternak)
      191, 201
Donskoi Monastery 181, 187

Dostovevsky, Fyodor 178
Drake, Ted 20, 26
Driberg, Tom 156
Dubcek, Alexander 69, 98, 204
Dukhon, Boris 151–2
Dunning, Eric 88
Dutt, Rajani Palme 53

Edelman, Robert 88
Eisenhower, President 3
Enemy Within: The Rise and Fall of
      the British Communist Party
      (Beckett) 80–1
Engels, Friedrich 203

Falber, Reuben 80
Falin, Yuri 144
Ferrier, Harry 21
Finland 66, 116
Flewin, Reg 20, 21
Flynn, Paddy 46
football:
   as an expression of
      non-conformity among
      Soviet people 3–4, 5
   Bradford fire 208–9
   Heysel tragedy 209
   JR plays at university 50–1
   JR plays for British Diplomatic
      Corps 90–1, 126, 129, 132, 133
   JR plays for Moscow Spartak see
      Moscow Spartak
   JR's early love of 26–7
   JR plays in armed forces 41, 45–6
   politics and see Nikolai Starostin
      and Moscow Spartak
   Soviet see Soviet Union
   stadiums 89–90
   violence 207–8
   see also under individual
      club name
Football Association 19, 42

Forehead, Ted 31
Foreman, Chas 31
Foster, William Z. 67–8
Francis, Ben 166
Franco, General 191
Fratton Park, Portsmouth 27, 120, 138, 153
Frayn, Michael 38
French Communist Party 70, 98
Frogatt, Jack 21
Fryer, Peter 53
Futbol skvoz gody (*Football Through the Years*) 179

Gagarin, Yuri 70, 72, 78, 119
Georgia 111–12, 187
Gollan, John 69–70
Gorbachov, Mikhail 150, 179, 211
Gorelkin, Ivan 188
Gorky, Maxim 39, 51, 109
Goulden, Len 24
Granin, Nikolai 72
Great Terror 99, 174, 179, 186, 201
    see also Stalin, Joseph
Great Terror, The (Conquest) 174
Griffiths, Wyn 25
Gromyko, Andrei 118
Grossman, Vasily 115
gulags 82–3, 178–9, 180–2, 191–2
Guthrie, Jimmy 20, 23

Halifax, Lord 105
Hall, Gus 98
Halton, Reg 20, 25
Hanna, Anna 101, 102
Hanna, George 100–2, 104, 120, 159, 171
Hanna, Lucy 101, 102
Hanna, Rose 101
Harfield, Frank 'Pimple' 31
Harris, John 24
Harris, Peter 20, 21, 143

Heath, Edward 165
Heysel Stadium tragedy 209
Higher Party School *see* Moscow Higher Party School
Hines, Barry 52
Hitler, Adolf 41, 42, 43, 113, 114, 191
Hobsbawn, Eric 53
Holmes, 'Zigger' 22
Hungarian uprising 1956 53, 54, 157, 174, 175

Ibarurri, Dolores 70
Ilyushin, Vladimir 72
Infernal Grove, The (Muggeridge) 163
International Brigade 52, 86, 98
International Lenin School 64, 71, 98, 99, 101
Invergordon Mutiny 102, 120
Isaacs, Bernard 101, 120

James, Alex 22
Johnstone, Archie 158, 166
Joint Services School for Linguists, Cornwall 36–40

Kairat FC 148, 193
Kassil, Lev 86
Kavazashvili, Anzor 202
Kerr, Sir Archibald Clark 163
Kerrigan, Peter 98
KGB 174, 201
Kharchenko, Ivan 183
Khomich, 'Tiger' 121
Khrushchov, Nikita 2, 3, 49, 53, 54, 63, 71, 82–3, 103, 116, 118–19, 137, 139, 151, 157, 171, 174–5, 178
Khusainov, Galimzhan 87, 153–4, 202
Klugmann, James 73–4, 162, 163
Knopova, E. L. 194

Komsomol 184, 187, 211

Kosarev, Alexander 183, 184, 186, 187, 189, 194

Kostomarov, Vitaly 70

Koutaissov, Elizabeth 48, 49

Labour Party (UK) 23, 30, 54

Lawton, Tommy 24, 25, 26, 140

Lazurkina, D. A. 68

Lee, Johnner 31

'Lend-Lease' agreement (US–UK) 38, 81

l'Etoile Rouge 2, 185

Lenin Stadium 1, 2, 87, 89, 90, 126, 128, 129, 133, 138, 144, 147, 152, 195, 212 *see also* Olympic Stadium

Lenin, Vladimir Ilyich 2, 48, 68, 82, 109–10, 125, 179, 186, 195

Leuta, Stanislav 189

Lipton, Colonel Marcus 165

Lockhart, Robert Bruce 94, 96

Logofet, Gennady 87, 92, 129–30, 131, 132, 134, 141, 145, 146–7, 151, 177, 178, 202

London Institute of Education 56

Look Back in Anger (Osbourne) 52

Lubyanka 181, 189

Lysenko, Timofei 123

Macdonald, Ramsay 161

Maclean, Donald 1, 74, 91, 120, 123, 126, 156, 157, 159–60, 161–5, 168–9, 170–3

Maclean, Melinda 126, 158, 170, 171, 172

Macmillan, Harold 165

Manchester Communist Party Archive 69–70, 72

Mandaric, Milan 153

Mandelshtam, Osip 178, 182

Manning, L. V. 25

Mapryal Russian Language Organisation 70

Marshak, Samuel 116, 118

Marshall Plan 81

Marx, Groucho 6

Marx, Karl 96, 125, 181, 199, 203

Marxism 49, 50, 71, 128, 162, 163, 174

Marxism Today 74

Matthews, George 80, 205

Matthews, Stanley 25, 42, 120

McNeil, Hector 164

Meyerhold, Vsevolod 180–1

MI5 64, 81, 164, 165

MI6 163, 164

Mikoyan, Anastas 118

Milchakov, Alexander 187

Miller, Arthur 45

Mills, Henry 30

Modin, Yuri 171

Moffat, Alec 98

Moffatt, Keith 172

Molchanov, Alexander 73, 74, 198–9

Molotov, Prime Minister 51, 180, 188

Montagu, Ivor 43, 54–5

Montgomery, General 19

Morgan, Lew 20

Morning Star 81, 116

Morozov, Saava 91

Mortensen, Stan 25

Moscow Art Theatre 118

Moscow City Council 145

Moscow Dinamo 120, 121, 210
  Beria and 187–8
  founded 184
  Nikolai Starostin and 191, 192, 193
  rivalry with Moscow Spartak 88, 148, 149, 153, 184–5
  secret-service club 88, 184, 191
  UK tour 1945 23–6, 86, 121

Moscow Higher Party School
    (HPS) 1, 2, 49, 115–17,
    148, 197, 198, 199, 204, 205,
    211, 212
  CPGB and 69–70, 81, 97
  families, treatment of members
    107–10
  function of 64–9, 75, 91
  JR completes course 124, 127
  JR's silence concerning time at 154
  origins of 97–8
  sport and 85–6
Moscow News 126
Moscow Public University 64
Moscow Radio 56, 99, 100,
    103, 200
Moscow Spartak 5, 128, 207, 210
  cup victory 1939 188
  fans 86
  history of 183–96
  JR plays for 1, 2, 3, 6, 40, 133–46,
    148–9, 177, 197
  JR revisits team-mates 2005 150–4
  JR trains with 129–32, 147
  JR watches 86, 91, 202
  name 183
  Nikolai Starostin and 2, 128, 130,
    135, 177–89, 194–6
  sports society 128–9
  style of play 86–7
  Supporters Club 151–2
Mosfilm 103
Muggeridge, Malcolm 163

Nagy, Imre 204
Nasser, President 52
Nazi Party 41, 42, 43, 77, 89,
    102, 103
Netto, Igor 87, 134, 135–6, 138,
    139, 141, 143, 147, 148,
    149–50, 153, 202
Netto, Lev 136

Nevsky 95, 96
NKVD 188
Novy Mir 178

Ogden, Dennis 72–3, 118,
    158–9, 169
Okudzhava, Bulat 178
Olympic Stadium 153, 154 *see also*
    Lenin Stadium
Olympics 55, 128
  1936 41
  1938 42
  1952 77–8, 121, 145
  1955 43
*One Day in the Life of Ivan
    Denisovich* (Solzhenitsin) 178
Orton, Hilda 50
Orwell, George 51, 110
Osbourne, John 52

Pakhtakor 137, 140, 144–5
Parker, Cliff 20
Pasternak, Boris 191, 201
Pavlov, Sergei 124
Paynter, Will 98
Perham, Hilda 157
Philby, Kim 74, 91, 157, 161, 162–3,
    164, 165, 172, 173–4, 175
Phillips, Len 21
Pilnyak, Boris 182
Pollitt, Harry 69, 80, 101–2, 105
Popov, Pyotr 189
Portsmouth Dockyard 16, 28
Portsmouth Dockyard League
    138, 149
Portsmouth Football Club 5, 12,
    19–23, 47, 63, 87, 89, 143, 202,
    206–8, 209–10
Portsmouth Southern Grammar
    School 28–31, 54
Potter, Dennis 38
Powell, Robert Baden 94

Powers, Gary 3
'Prague Spring' 204
Professional Footballers'
    Association (PFA) 23
Progress Publishers 2, 100, 117,
    124–5, 127, 128, 200, 201
Prokofiev, Victor 185
Prokopovich, S. N. 49
Putin, Vladimir 211

RAF Gatow 45
Real Madrid 89–90
Red Army 38, 115, 180, 183
Redknapp, Harry 206
Reid, Betty 57, 69, 71, 84
Reid, Dougie 21
Reilly, Sidney 93–4, 126
Reingold, Valery 87, 139, 143,
    144, 149
Riordan, Annick (first wife) 8,
    59–60, 62, 64, 67, 71, 86, 107,
    126–7, 170, 197
Riordan, Catherine (daughter) 206
Riordan, James 'Kit' (grandfather)
    7, 8–9
Riordan, James William 'Jim':
  British Communist Party,
    relationship with 54, 57, 81,
    84, 104–6, 117, 123–4, 197,
    202–5
  British-Soviet Friendship Society
    and 55–6, 120
  childhood 7–17, 19–31
  class awareness 1, 30–1, 51–2, 56,
    163, 175
  Communist sympathies, growth
    of 4–5, 44, 49–50, 51–2, 53–7,
    123–4, 174
  doubts concerning Soviet system
    83, 123–4, 198–201
  denied re-entry visa to Soviet
    Union 201–2

doctoral dissertation on Soviet
    sport 92, 127–9, 197
early jobs 33–4
father, relationship with 7–8,
    9, 47
football and 26–7, 41, 45–6,
    50–1, 85–6, 90–1, 126, 129,
    132, 133 see also Moscow
    Spartak and Portsmouth
    Football Club
languages, talent for 30
lecturer in Russian Studies,
    Bradford University 205–6
left wing causes, supports
    52, 56
London, moves to 56–7
love life see Riordan, Annick and
    Riordan, Rashida
Moscow, first visits 55–6
Moscow Higher Party School,
    involvement with 1, 2, 49,
    64–75, 81, 85–6, 91, 97–8,
    107–11, 115–17, 124, 127, 148,
    154, 197, 198, 199, 204, 205,
    211, 212
mother, relationship with 1, 7–8,
    9, 13–14, 15, 16, 17, 27, 28, 31,
    44, 47, 63, 109, 110, 166
National Service 1, 26, 33–40,
    41–6, 51, 59, 74, 131
pacifism 37
RAF 34–40, 41–6, 53, 159
return to England 197–204
Russian language, learns 1, 26,
    37, 38–9, 48–50
Soviet Union, first visit to 55–6
teacher, trains to be a 56
teddy boy 52
'The Growing Pains of Soviet
    Youth' 199–200
translator 124–7, 197, 206
university 30, 46–51

Riordan, Nadine (daughter) 127, 197, 206
Riordan, Nathalie (daughter) 206
Riordan, Rashida (second wife) 206
Riordan, Sean (son) 206, 209
Riordan, Tania (daughter) 62, 107, 108, 109, 122, 197, 206, 209, 211
Roca, Blas 70
Rochet, Waldeck 98
Rochford, Bill 20
Rodichenko, Vladimir 192
Rooke, Ronnie 25
Rookes, Phil 20
Rothstein, Andrew 103
Rozhdestvensky, Robert 178
Russell, Billy 54
Russian Journal (Steinbeck) 45–6
Russian Orthodox Church 151, 211
Rust, Bill 98

Salazar, Antonio 64
Scoular, Jimmy 21
Sdobnikov, Yuri 128–9
Service, Robert 82, 179
Shankly, Bill 5
Shanyavsky, A. L. 64
Shaw, George Bernard 110
Shostakovich, Dmitri 86, 117
Sillitoe, Alan 52
Simonyan, Nikita 2, 129, 130, 132–4, 137, 143, 144, 147, 148, 202
Sloan, Pat 199
Smertin, Alexei 150, 195–6, 210
Smith, George (grandfather) 9, 11–13, 24
Smith, Grandma (grandmother) 9
Snegov, Colonel 188
Solzhenitsin, Alexander 178
Sovetov, Krylya 193

Soviet union:
    British Diplomatic Corps in 90–1, 126, 129, 132, 133
    corruption in 82
    cricket in 155–60
    darker side to life in 122
    drunkenness in 82
    effect of World War II upon 78–9, 114–15
    football in 3–4, 85–96, 120–1, 129–54, 182–96
    industrial growth 81–2
    interpretation of history 74–5
    living standards in 123–4
    Mongol-Tatar invasion 49
    Revolution 1917 49, 93, 183
    Seven-Year Plan 1959 81–2
    sport in 77–8, 127–9, 183, 184 *see also* football
    suspicion of foreigners inside 2–3, 101, 137
    see also Communist Party of the Soviet Union
Soviet Young Communists 56
Spanish Civil War 52, 70, 86, 99, 162
Spender, Stephen 162
Sport 95
Spy Who Betrayed a Generation, The (Page/Leitch/Knightley) 160, 163
Stalin, Joseph 50, 51, 55, 80, 82, 88, 103, 123, 124, 178
    character 23
    death 2, 137, 180, 193
    Khrushchov's criticism of 63, 68–9, 82, 157, 174–5
    preserved body 68, 122
    purges and crimes 1, 23, 49, 53, 56, 71, 75, 99–106, 116, 126, 128, 136, 170, 174–5, 179–83, 186, 198, 199, 201, 203, 211

  sport and 139
  writings 44
  Yugoslavia and 121
St Catherine Nunnery 181
St Petersburg Cricket and Lawn
    Tennis Club 93, 155
St Petersburg League 95
Stalin, Vasily 192–3
Stalingrad 114–15
Stanley, Brian 31
Starostin, Alexander 183,
    189–91, 194
Starostin, Andrei 178–9, 183,
    189–91, 194
Starostin, Nikolai 2, 128, 130, 135,
    177–96
Starostin, Pyotr 183, 189–90, 191,
    194–5
Starostin, Yevgenia 193
State Order of Lenin Institute of
    Physical Culture 92
Stoklitsky, Len 101, 120, 126
Streltsov, Eduard 143
Suez Crisis 52, 53

Taylor, Jim 24
Tereshkova, Valentina 78, 119
Thatcher, Margaret 208
Theatre Royal, Portsmouth 16
Thomas, D. M. 38, 39
Thomas, Derek 31
Thompson, Professor George
    49–50
Thorez, Maurice 70, 80
Tikston, Pavel 189
Timofeyevna, Valentina 108
Tinn, Jack 19
Tito, Josip Broz 98, 121
Togliatti, Palmiro 80

Tolstoy, Count Leo 130, 146
Trifonov, Yuri 86
Trotsky, Leon 56, 67, 72, 203
Tsvetayeva, Marina 178

Usov, Nikolai 188
Utley, Freda 105
U-2 spy plane 3
Utyosov, Leonid 86

Vegoda, Jeff 206
Victoria 94–5, 96
Vietnam War 52, 56
Voznesensky, Andrei 116, 178

Walker, Harry 20
Wall, Sir Frederick 42–3
Waterhouse, Keith 52
Watson, Ian 31
West Ham United 43
Wheeler, Terry 31
Wilson, Harold 49
Wincott, Len 102–4, 119–20, 171
World War II 2, 7, 9, 11–17, 78,
    100, 101, 114, 164, 192

Yakushin, Mikhail 26
Yashin, Lev 120–1
Yeltsin, Boris 195, 211
Yevtushenko, Yevgeny 116, 178
Yezhov, Nikolai 181
Young Communist League
    60, 183

Zedong, Mao 79
Zhivkov, Todor 79–80
Zhmelnikov, Vladislav 186
Znamensky, Georgi 185–6
Znamensky, Serafim 185–6

What's next?

Tell us the name of an author you love

and we'll find your next great book.

www.bookarmy.com